KUSINA NI EC

OVER 200 EVERYDAY RECIPES

Eufemia C. Estrada

ANVIL

Published and exclusively distributed by
ANVIL PUBLISHING, INC.
2/F Team Pacific Building
13 Jose Cruz St., Bo. Ugong
Pasig City, Philippines
Telephones 671-1899 • 671-1888
Fax 671-9235

First Printing, 1997
Second Printing, June 1998
Third Printing, November 1998

Art Direction by *Albert Gamos*
Cover Design by *Ricardo Montezon*
Illustrations by *Ed Gamos*

ISBN 971-27-0682-6

Printed by
MG Reprographics, Inc.
7-1 Villamor St., San Juan, Metro Manila

TO MY READERS —
OF 'KUSINA NI EC'
AND 'COOKING MADE EC'

Kusina ni EC

FOREWORD

One afternoon so long ago, I gave a lecture on feature writing before the usual mix of professionals, writers and writers-to-be. At the end of this lively but tiring session where I was asked just about every question on mass media from how to meet deadlines to why People's Journal's banners were like that this petite woman with salt-and-pepper hair and harmless grin walked up to me, her hand thrusting a sheet of bond paper into my hand. On such a moment, any editor could sniff instantly an unsolicited manuscript.

She was a retired public school teacher, this woman told me. She wrote on the side and right now she had an article which I might read and run in my Lifestyle section. Where teachers are concerned, retired or otherwise, I show nothing short of respect. So with my chronic respect for teachers, I accepted what was being given and gave an editor's stock answer: I'll call you (translation: don't call me).

Back in the office, I scanned the manuscript, which turned out to be one of the most heartwarming and comic essays I had read that week. Any writer who could make a jaded editor laugh makes a fine contributor. I don't even remember now what that essay was about must

Kusina ni EC

have been about a retiree's life, or a retiree's inability to stand commuter traffic. What I do remember is the essayist's wit particularly that rare ability of a single woman past mid-life (okay, a spinster) to laugh at herself.

From that moment on, Eufemia C. Estrada became my Lifestyle contributor, unreliable contributor. She wrote when she felt like it, called you whenever a story idea struck her, promised you a submission date while you bought her story idea but never believed her promise. Fine arrangement.

Oh but when she did deliver, you had engaging pieces. Ms. Estrada wrote for me a bag of topics, from her arthritis to life with her nieces and nephews.

This unreliable contributor followed me to wherever my career took me, significantly to Manila Chronicle. In time, Ms. Estrada became EC to me and my staff who, harassed by deadlines and the challenge to constantly innovate, had no second to waste calling her by her long name whenever we followed up her articles.

In time the way we called her EC changed from the professional to the personal. We called her EC now in a most familiar way for by this time, she was family to us. Why?

Here comes a most significant part of the story. She had begun sending us her homemade cookies and cakes. They were not only yummy, *they were also treasures, especially when we felt famished on those long Friday nights.*

We had discovered that EC could bake and cook wondrously enough to satisfy a starved staff whose deadline she could evade. Yes, you could say EC sometimes baked her way out of a deadline. (Deadline was negotiable when you had EC cookies waiting for you.)

And that was how EC the Food Columnist was born.

Her Kusina ni EC became Cooking Made EC when I moved to Philippine Daily Inquirer in 1994. I brought along EC to my new home because I was certain that Inquirer's wide readership would benefit greatly from her home-spun recipes. I was right. She gets her share of readers' mail, and she now writes for a monthly glossy magazine, Food.

And surprise, she hardly misses a deadline.

Now we have the best of both worlds: EC meeting her weekly deadline, and EC sending us her home-made specialities on special occasions.

THELMA S. SAN JUAN

❊❊❊❊❊

PREFACE

I never planned a second trajectory after retirement. It just happened.

I met Thelma S. San Juan in a journalism seminar when I was 50 and got started on feature writing as a free lancer. After almost a decade, when arthritis began to slow me down, I opted for optional retirement from my teaching position. Thelma, who knew I was a baking and cooking enthusiast, suggested I write a cooking column for Chronicle where she was then Lifestyle editor.

Maybe it's not quite right to say it just happened, for through all my early adult years I had been honing my baking and cooking skills by taking lessons from well-known culinary experts — Nora Daza, Doña Lola Lobregat, Victoria Limjuco Dayrit, Constancia Maramag, Dexter Rebolledo among others.

While my associates taught in private schools as a sideline, I baked cakes for friends and their families and friends. I also took graduate studies in English Literature and Journalism but without aiming for a degree. It was a happy and satisfying blend of intellectual and creative pursuits.

When I was up for promotion, my boss told our schools superintendent that my baking, in particular, was the equivalent of a master's degree, considered a must in the academe. (I got the promotion anyway.)

This two-volume cookbook covers the period from April 1991 to late 1994 when I was with the

Chronicle. The first volume covers soups to main dishes. The second volume will cover meal endings. The recipes featured come from various sources — books, magazines and newspaper clippings dating from the 50's, treasured personal collections of family, friends and cooks of friends, government and private agencies engaged in food and nutrition research, even total strangers who had interesting recipes to share.

Aside from Thelma who started everything, I thank the following:

The Chronicle for three and a half years of mutual benefit

My friend Larry Canlas, now of L.A., for the many years' supply of US magazines wherein I made countless culinary discoveries

My family, friends and even strangers who generously shared their "trade secrets"

My readers who let me know by word of mouth or through their letters that my column was filling up a real need

My nephews Raymund Deleña and Ed Estrada and my niece Maya Estrada for encoding the manuscript

And Karina Bolasco of Anvil for encouraging me to compile my columns into a book.

Maraming salamat!

EUFEMIA C. ESTRADA

Kusina ni EC

TABLE OF CONTENTS

Part I

Kusina ni EC

Part 1

Soups

The secret of this family recipe for Pancit Molo is lots of garlic, in the filling and in the soup.

Pancit Molo

Filling:
1/4 kilo ground pork, *lomo*
1/4 kilo fresh shrimp, peeled and chopped
1/2 chicken breast, boiled and chopped fine
1 cup *apulid* or *singkamas*, chopped fine
1 whole head garlic, minced
1 egg
Salt and pepper to taste

Soup:
Soup stock (from soup bones and 1 chicken breast)
1 head garlic, minced
1 onion, sliced
Patis and pepper to taste
Green onions, finely chopped
1/2 chicken breast, cooked and flaked
Wonton wrappers, cut in half to form triangles

Mix filling ingredients well. Wrap in *wonton* wrapper and set aside. This can be made ahead and frozen till needed.

To wrap filling: Using your small finger, place about 1/4 teaspoon of filling on top of the triangle. Fold twice toward the base. Pick up one end and fold it diagonally over the mound of filling and fold the other end to overlap it. Seal ends with a dab of water.

Form any leftover filling into half-inch balls.

Sauté onion in hot oil. Add flaked chicken, the soup stock (strained) and the minced garlic. Let boil briskly. Add the wrapped *molo* into the soup stock one at a time. Add the unwrapped balls too. It's done when the *molo* float. Season with *patis* and pepper. Serve hot with a sprinkling of green onions.

Pancit Lang-Lang is a specialty the town of Imus is known for. This recipe is from Bella Espiritu who learned it from her husband Dr. Romeo Espiritu who hails from the town.

Pancit Lang-Lang

1/2 kilo *bijon* (*primera*)
1/4 kilo sirloin
1/4 kilo medium size shrimp
4 duck's eggs
1 piece beef bone
Green onions
Toasted garlic

Ground pepper
Patis, vetsin and salt

Boil 2 eggs and set aside.

Boil the sirloin and pork until tender. Boil the soup bone in enough water for the soup. If you wish you may boil the bone, beef and pork together to save on fuel.

Shell the shrimps, slice into halves then cook into an omelet using the remaining duck eggs. To cook into omelet, beat eggs slightly, add enough cornstarch to make a medium-thick consistency, add the shrimp and cook in batches for the omelet. Don't forget to season with salt and pepper. Cut cooked omelet into 1/2 inch cubes. Cut boiled beef and pork also into cubes. Set aside.

Slice the 2 boiled eggs lengthwise. Chop the green onions and set aside.

Parboil the *bijon*, taking care not to overcook it or it will become mushy. Arrange the *bijon* in a large serving bowl. Top with beef, pork, shrimp omelet, boiled eggs, garlic, and green onions. Sprinkle with pepper.

Boil the soup stock and pour over the prepared *bijon* mixture just before serving. Season with *patis* and *vetsin* to taste. Prepare only enough for the crowd to be served. Prepare a fresh batch when you need more.

This goes very well with *biscocho* or toasted *pan de sal*.

Corn Chowder

2 tablespoons chopped onion
1/2 cup diced peeled potato
1 can cream-style corn
1/3 cup white sauce mix (See Ready Mixes
    page 234.)
1 cup milk
Salt and pepper to taste

Cook onion and potatoes in small amount of water till tender and water has evaporated. Add the corn, white sauce mix and milk and cook till thickened. Season with salt and pepper. Makes two cups.

Clam Chowder

2 tablespoons chopped onion
1/2 cup diced peeled potatoes
1 cup minced cooked clams
Pinch of thyme
1/3 cup white sauce mix
1 cup milk
Pepper to taste

Follow the same procedure as that for corn chowder.

Chicken Corn Chowder

4 cups chicken broth
2 cups chopped cooked chicken
1 can cream-style corn
1 teaspoon salt
1/4 teaspoon pepper
1 1/4 cups white sauce mix

In a large saucepan, stirring occasionally, heat all ingredients except mix. Add mix. Stir over low heat about 5 minutes or until thick and smooth.

Salads

❄❄❄❄

Pako Salad

Pako, cut and boiled
Tomatoes, sliced
Onions, sliced into rings
Hard-boiled eggs, sliced
Boiled potatoes, cut into cubes
Vinegar, sugar, pepper

Arrange *pako* on serving platter. Top with sliced tomatoes and onions, cubed potatoes and sliced hard-boiled eggs. Serve with a vinegar-sugar-pepper dressing.

Similar to this is a *Kangkong* Salad another friend, Elayda Marasigan, shared with me.

Kangkong Salad

Kangkong
Onions, tomatoes, hard-boiled eggs, boiled
    potatoes
Vinegar, salt, sugar, pepper

Boil *kangkong* quickly. Arrange on a platter. Top with sliced tomatoes, onions, potatoes cut into cubes, and hard-boiled eggs.

Serve with a dressing of vinegar, salt, pepper, and mashed egg yolk.

A version of *Puso* Salad is a favorite of my cousin Maria who is from Zamboanga.

Puso Salad

Puso ng saging, preferably *saba*
Onions, salt, pepper, ginger, vinegar, and
       fresh *gata*

Remove outer leaves of *puso* leaving only the tender core. Boil till tender. Cut fine. Squeeze out liquid.

Serve with onions and a dressing of vinegar, salt, pepper, finely minced ginger, and fresh *gata*. Mix it all up.

Every time I see *katuray* blossoms in the market or on provincial trips, I am reminded of my mother. She just loved *katuray* salad though I was not adventurous enough to try it. But when I had taken over the marketing and cooking chores, I always got her some *katuray* whenever they were available.

Katuray Salad

Katuray flowers, pink or white
Vinegar, salt, and pepper

Remove bitter stamens from *katuray* flowers.
Blanch. Serve with a vinegar-salt-pepper dressing.

Only recently, my cousin Nony gave me a big bundle
of *pechay* Tagalog freshly picked from his front lawn
garden. Having just finished a supply of this vegetable,
I wondered aloud how I could prepare it differently
from my tried and tired ways.

My aunt came to the rescue with a raw *pechay*
salad. Preparing it is easier than pie. I guess it's safe to
eat it raw when you know its source.

Pechay Salad

Wash the *pechay* very well. Cut into one-inch
pieces, separating the stalks from the leaves. Separate
stalks and leaves and squeeze very well.

I served it with a dressing of cider vinegar and
honey. It was just like the more popular lettuce we
know.

Sweet Potato Chicken Salad

1 kilo sweet potatoes
1 medium-size onion
1 medium-size can pineapple chunks
2 chicken breasts, cooked and shredded
2 medium-size carrots
1/4 kilo Baguio beans, parboiled
1/4 cup vinegar
1/4 teaspoon pepper
Lettuce leaves

Boil sweet potatoes, then add carrots. Do not overcook. Dice, including raw onion. Slice pineapple into cubes and mix with above ingredients. Add salad dressing, vinegar and pepper. Chill 2 hours or more. Serve on lettuce leaves.

Party Chicken Salad

1/4 cup vegetable oil
1/4 cup orange marmalade
3 tablespoons cider vinegar
3 tablespoons mayonnaise
2 teaspoons curry powder
1/4 teaspoon salt
6 cups cubed cooked chicken

2 tablespoons golden raisins
2 tablespoons sliced almonds
2 tablespoons chopped parsley

Mix all ingredients well. Garnish with orange slices.

Fish Salad

Any white fish (*bangus* will do)
Mayonnaise
1 apple, pared, cored and cubed
Raisins
Salt and pepper to taste

Cook the *bangus*, debone flesh and flake. Cool.
Add the rest of the ingredients and mix well. Chill.

If desired, save the fish head (cooked) and use it in serving the salad. Place the fish head on one end of the platter and arrange the salad in the shape of a fish body. Garnish with sections of chopped hard-boiled eggs, chopped carrots, chopped pimiento, pickle relish.

Buko Salad

2 cups *buko*
1/2 cup cooked ham, cut into strips
1/2 cup chicken breast, cooked and flaked
1 can pineapple tidbits, drained
1/4 cup grated cheese
1 cup mayonnaise
1/2 cup sweet pickle relish

Mix all ingredients and chill before serving.

Beef

❄❄❄❄

During my growing up years, I didn't have to look at a calendar to tell Sundays. *Cocido* on the dining table was a sure sign.

My role was to go to my *Ninang's* house next door to buy one *chorizo bilbao* (*Marca El Rey*) which she bought by the can, and grind a bowl of ripe tomatoes on her manual grinder for the sauce.

Cocido

1 whole piece of *kenchi* (*sa una*), whole or
    sliced, one-inch thick
1 *chorizo bilbao*
1 slice salt pork or 1 piece ham hock
1 piece *bulalo* (also called *tuhod*)
Cabbage
Pechay
Camote
Bananas (*saba*)
Chick peas (*garbanzos* soaked overnight) or
White beans (soaked overnight)
Peppercorns
Tomatoes, ripe, seeded and finely chopped
Eggplants, whole, peeled just before using
Garlic

In a big casserole, cook the *kenchi*, salt pork and *bulalo* in just enough water to cover. Skim off the scum before the water boils. Add the *chorizo bilbao*, chick peas or white beans and simmer till tender. Set aside the *kenchi*.

In the broth, add the *camote* and bananas and when these are half-cooked, add the cabbage, cut up, and lastly the *pechay*. Cook only till vegetables are crisp.

Cook the sauce.

Tomato sauce: Saute some garlic, chopped onions and the tomatoes. Simmer till the tomatoes are cooked. Season to taste. If sauce gets too dry, add a little broth and let boil awhile.

Eggplant sauce: Add the peeled eggplant to the broth together with the other vegetables. Carefully remove the cooked eggplant. Mash with a fork. Add vinegar to taste and lots of finely pounded garlic.

Add a little sugar and salt to taste.

To serve: Arrange the beef and the vegetables on serving platter.

Serve the soup separately, either plain or cooked with some noodles.

The *Cocido*, *Sinigang na Karne* and *Kalitiran* are my mother's recipes. For the *Sinigang* she used that part of the brisket with a layer of hard fat which was just great when cooked. The *Kalitiran* could pass for tongue and makes a festive dish.

Sinigang na Karne

1 kilo *punta y pecho* (brisket)
Tomatoes, sliced
Onions, sliced
Cabbage, cut into large chunks
Pechay, cut into 1-inch pieces
Radish, cut into rounds
Eggplant
Sitao, cut into 2-inch pieces and tied together
    in bunches
Sampaloc
Salt to taste

Cook the beef, tomatoes and onions together. Cook over a slow fire, stirring occasionally, until the beef is slightly brown. Add enough rice washing to cook the beef till it's tender and still have enough soup to cook the vegetables in.

Put the *sampaloc* in a *katsa* bag, add it to the pot and when the *sampaloc* is soft, mash it to extract the juice.

If you wish, you may remove the beef from the pot and cook the vegetables separately, starting with the ones which take longer to cook. Do not overcook the vegetables. You may use all the vegetables mentioned or use only a few of your choice. Check the seasoning. Serve hot with *patis* and *calamansi*. Take care to serve this piping hot or the soup may set into *sebo*. To avoid this, you may tenderize the beef the day before serving, refrigerate, and take out the fat that forms on top of the mixture.

Mother's *Kalitiran*

1 whole *kalitiran* (from 1 to 1 3/4 kilos
     depending on size)
Salt
Pepper
Cooking oil
Laurel leaf
Whole pepper (peppercorns)
Flour
1 onion, minced
Worcestershire Sauce
Potatoes, quartered or half-inch strips
Carrots, cut into chunks
1 can whole kernel corn
Sweet garden peas

Rub the *kalitiran* with salt and ground pepper. Let stand for a while.

Heat a little oil in a skillet or saucepan and when it's very hot, brown the meat on all sides over a hot fire to seal in the juices.

Drain the oil and in the same pan cook the meat in a little water (just enough to cook it till tender) with a little salt, laurel leaf and peppercorns. Simmer till tender.

Cool and refrigerate overnight for easier handling.

To prepare the dish, slice the *kalitiran* as thinly as possible. Remove fat from liquid.

Brown the onion, put it aside, and brown about two heaping tablespoonfuls of all-purpose flour in the same pan. Add the liquid in which the meat was cooked, stirring to avoid lumps. Simmer then add the meat slices gently and simmer for a little while. Season to taste.

To serve: arrange the meat slices on a platter the way you serve your ox tongue. Spoon some of the gravy over it. Serve with fried potatoes, buttered carrots, whole kernel corn, sweet garden peas.

Mely's Beef *Afritada*

1 piece *kalitiran*, cubed
Onion, sliced
Tomatoes, sliced
Salt and pepper
Vinegar, just a little
Soy sauce
Little sugar

Cook *kalitiran* in onion, tomatoes, salt and pepper, vinegar, soy sauce until tender. Sauté more garlic, onion, tomato sauce and tomato paste, a little sugar and add beef. Strain sauce where beef was boiled and add to the rest of the mixture.

Garnish with fried potatoes or green pepper. Or add carrots and sweet peas to beef.

Note: For every kilo of beef add 3/4 cup water for tenderizing.

The Alcabaos of Ayala, Alabang just love this Korean stew my cousin Med makes especially for picnics. The trouble, the family says, is, "You know Mama. When we like a dish she makes it and makes it till we get tired of it." The Beefsteak Tagalog is also Med's.

Korean Stew

Short ribs
Rice wine
Soy sauce
Water
Salt
Ginger
Sugar
Baguio leeks
Sesame seeds, toasted

Day before, cook the short ribs in a mixture of

rice wine, soy sauce, water, salt and ginger until tender. Cool and refrigerate overnight. The following day, remove fat that has solidified on top.

In a saucepan, cook the short ribs adding sugar and Baguio leeks. When ribs are tender and the sauce has thickened, add the toasted sesame seeds.

Beefsteak Tagalog

1 kilo beef (*batok* with *butong mura*)
1 cup water
1/4 cup *toyo*
Laurel leaf
Juice from 5 *calamansi*
2 big white onions, sliced into rings

Slice beef across the grain finger-thick (thicker than for *tapa*) and cut into 2-inch lengths.

Cook in a saucepan with water, the *toyo* and laurel leaf.

When the beef is almost tender, add *calamansi* juice and just before you take it from the fire, add the sliced onion and cook only till crisp. Serve hot.

Maruja Herrera cooks up this Osso Buco for special guests.

Osso Buco

1 kilo veal knuckle or shank
3/4 cup seasoned flour (with salt and
    pepper), for
    dredging
8 tablespoons butter or margarine or corn oil
1 can peeled tomatoes
1 large onion, thinly sliced in rings
4 tablespoons tomato paste
1/4 cup dry white wine (not sweet)
Salt and pepper to taste
1 teaspoon sugar

Dredge meat in flour; shake off excess. Melt butter in a large, shallow casserole. Brown meat lightly and evenly. Transfer to plate. Add onion to casserole and fry till soft. Stir in tomatoes and juice in can and tomato paste and cook for 3 minutes. Pour over the wine, add salt and pepper and sugar and bring to boil. Return meat to casserole and mix well. Reduce heat to low. Cover and simmer for 2 to 2 1/2 hours or until meat is almost falling off the bone.

Meanwhile, make Gremolata: Combine 1 tablespoon finely grated lemon rind, 6 pieces garlic cloves, minced, and 1 1/2 tablespoons finely chopped parsley. Stir into meat mixture and cook for 1 minute.

Serves 6.

One way to cope with the rising cost of beef is to use it ground. Because it's ground, it stretches.

Your choice of ground beef will depend on your priorities. If cost is top priority, get the cheaper ground beef which contains more fat (and maybe *litid* too). If healthy eating is what counts, then opt for the less fatty kinds, like ground round or sirloin.

Then again, if you buy your beef in the wet markets, it would be best to choose your beef cut and have it ground for you. But if you go to a reputable supermarket for your beef, it's safe to get your beef pre-ground.

Use only freshly ground beef for your hamburger. I mix my hamburger, form the patties, and freeze these in single layers ready to use anytime I feel like eating a hamburger.

One of our family favorites is my mother's *Bola-bola* with Brown Sauce. To make her *bola-bola* tender, she used half beef, half pork. Usually *lomo* and ground round or sirloin. It's better tasting than using breadcrumbs or oatmeal in the mix.

Bola-bola with Brown Sauce

1/2 kilo lean ground beef
1/2 kilo ground pork *lomo*
2 big onions, minced
Salt and pepper
2 eggs

Cooking oil
Flour
Worcestershire sauce

Mix the first five ingredients till well-blended. Form into balls the size of walnuts.

Heat cooking oil till hot, add meatballs and reduce heat to cook through. Turn when necessary and cook till nicely brown. Drain well and set aside.

To make brown sauce:

Reduce fat in skillet where you cooked the meatballs. Brown flour and gradually add water and mix well to blend. Add Worcestershire sauce and simmer till smooth and slightly thick. Test for taste.

Add the cooked meatballs and simmer a while longer for sauce to penetrate.

Serve with any of the following: shoestring potatoes, sweet peas, sweet corn, boiled and buttered Baguio beans and carrots or mini corn.

Basic Meatballs

1/2 kilo ground round or sirloin
1/4 cup dried breadcrumbs
1 onion, finely chopped
1/2 cup milk
Ketchup
1 teaspoon salt

Pepper
Butter/margarine

Mix well all ingredients except the butter or margarine. Form into balls.

Sauté lightly in butter/margarine in skillet. Or bake, without butter, in shallow pan in preheated 375°F oven for 10 to 15 minutes or until cooked through.

Meatballs in Curry Sauce

1 can cream of mushroom soup, undiluted
1 tablespoon curry powder
3/4 cup raisins
1 teaspoon cider vinegar
Meatballs

In saucepan, mix well all ingredients except the meatballs. Bring to a boil. Reduce heat, add meatballs, cover and simmer till heated through.

Meatballs in Mushroom Gravy

Meatballs, browned in butter/margarine
Mushroom gravy: 1 can condensed golden
mushroom soup

Mix one can condensed mushroom soup with 1/3 cup water. Pour over meatballs in oven-proof casserole. Cover and bake in 375°F oven for 30 to 45 minutes.

Good with rice, mashed or baked potatoes.

Stews are hearty dishes and always a welcome item on one's menu. They can be made ahead and frozen too. Real handy when unexpected guests come.

To make a good stew it is necessary to coat the meat with seasoned flour and brown it in hot oil. This seals in the juices and ensures a dark brown crustiness. Besides, the crusty leftover in the pan used for browning adds flavor and color and thickens the sauce.

To flour the meat, put the seasoned flour in a plastic or brown bag or a bowl and shake or toss about half of the meat at time until pieces are separated and evenly coated with flour. Shake off excess flour into bag or bowl. Spread floured meat in a single layer on a sheet of waxed paper.

Tips for browning:

* Use the right pot, a 5- to 6-quart heavy, tightly lidded pot or Dutch oven preferably not aluminum unless it is non-stick.

* Heat oil over medium-high heat till it is thin and rippling but not smoking.

* Add meat in a single layer with room between pieces. Too many pieces at a time lowers the temperature of the oil and prevents browning.

* Browning takes 10 to 15 minutes per batch. Stir occasionally or turn large pieces to brown all sides.

* Remove each batch of browned meat and place in a plate or bowl.

* Reheat oil between batches.

Reheating:

Stews are even better the day after cooking. Remove solidified fat from top and start reheating over low heat, stirring often. As stew warms and liquefies increase heat to medium.

Flavoring:

A few drops of lemon juice or red wine vinegar added during the last 15 minutes of cooking adds flavor to the stew.

Use freshly ground pepper and fresh herbs whenever possible.

All-American Beef Stew

1 1/3 kilo well-trimmed beef round, cut into
    1/2-inch cubes
1/2 cup seasoned flour
1/3 cup vegetable oil
2 large onions, cut into wedges or thick
    rounds
4 medium-size carrots, cut in diagonal slices
    or into 1-inch lengths
1/2 kilo small red-skinned potatoes, quartered
3 ribs celery, cut into 1-inch lengths or slices
About 4 cups beef broth
2 tablespoons tomato paste
2 tablespoons Dijon mustard (optional)
1/2 teaspoon salt
Freshly ground pepper to taste

Coat meat with seasoned flour and brown in oil.
Remove meat to plate. Reduce heat to medium low.
Drain off all but 1 tablespoon pan drippings. Add
onions, carrots, potatoes and celery to pot. Cook until
lightly browned. Add broth, tomato paste and mustard,
stirring to scrape up browned bits. Bring to a boil.
Return browned meat to pot. Reduce heat. Cover and
simmer one hour. Check taste adding more broth and
salt and pepper if necessary. Cover and simmer one
hour longer, stirring once or twice until meat is tender
and sauce is slightly thickened.

Pork

❄❄❄❄

With improved methods of breeding, today's pork has less fat content. Closer trimming of fat means a healthier source of protein. Pork is also one of the best sources of thiamin and is rich in niacin, riboflavin and iron.

This casserole has become a family favorite since my sister discovered it in some book or magazine. It even won her a prize in a Maya Cookfest.

Hearty Ham Supper Dish

2 cups cubed ham
1 can canned whole corn kernels, drained
1 cup diced cooked potatoes
1/4 cup minced parsley
1 tablespoon finely chopped onion
1/4 teaspoon paprika
1/4 cup butter
1/4 cup all-purpose flour
2 cups milk
1 cup shredded cheese

In a 9x5-inch rectangular ovenproof glass dish, combine ham, corn kernels, potatoes, parsley, onion and paprika. Set aside.

Melt butter in a separate saucepan. Blend in flour and milk. Cook over medium heat, stirring constantly, until mixture thickens. Pour over ham mixture. Sprinkle grated cheese. Bake at 350°F for 20 to 30 minutes, or until golden brown.

Nanette Clarin, canteen manager of Manila High School for many years, who shares her recipes for Menudo I and Hamonado I uses *patis* instead of salt for seasoning. If you ask her why, she can only say, "*Basta*."

Pork *Hamonado*

1 kilo pork *pigue*
1 teaspoon *vetsin*
1/4 teaspoon Prague powder
1 cup sugar
1 tablespoon salt
1/2 bottle beer (drink the rest)
1/4 cup Ginebra gin
1 medium-size can crushed pineapple
1 bottle Sprite or Seven-Up
1 1/2 cups sugar

Slice the *pigue* as for *tapa*, taking care to keep it on one piece.

Rub well with a mixture of *vetsin*, Prague powder, salt, and sugar and marinate in refrigerator for 3 days – overnight, or just briefly, for rush orders.

Lay out the pork and spread center with contents of medium-size can of pineapple, roll tight and tie with string.

Cook in the mixture of beer, gin, more crushed pineapple together with its juice, Seven-Up or Sprite, a little water and sugar.

Cook till tender, taking care it doesn't scorch.

To serve: Let cool and slice into half-inch thickness. Remove string. Serve with sauce.

Pork *Hamonado* II

1 kilo pork
5 pieces *calamansi*
1 small can pineapple juice
4 tablespoons sugar
2 tablespoons salt
Ground pepper
Vetsin, if desired

Marinate pork in the rest of the ingredients overnight or at least one hour, if in a rush.

Brown the pork in oil, add the marinade and simmer till pork is tender. Turn off the heat as soon as the sauce thickens. (The sauce alone is *ulam na*, Pitching Jacob, Aling Anse's daughter, who shared this recipe with me, says.)

Conversing with cooking aficionados never fails to elicit interesting tips on the art.

Like roast beef turns out extra good when it is cooked in water till tender and in the marinade in which it is soaked.

This is how the late Lumen Briones of Pampanga used to prepare her roast beef or pork.

And for *lengua* she says that *lengua estofado* is different from *lengua estofada*. The latter has tomato sauce while the former is cooked with caramelized sugar and vinegar for a sweet sour taste.

In sautéing the garlic for the *lengua estofada* Lumen cautions not to brown the garlic as this will subtly change the flavor. She says this is one of the secrets of French cooking. And for the *estofado* Lumen prefers to use pork, the upper portion of the *pata*, rather than tongue.

Roast Pork or Beef

1 kilo *kasim* (pork butt) or *kalitiran* (beef)
Toyo
Calamansi
Garlic
Butter
Flour
Cream of mushroom
Button mushrooms

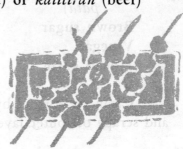

Have your meat dealer prepare the *kasim* for the roast. Or prepare it yourself. Cut off skin and part of the fat. Butterfly the meat, roll and tie with string at intervals.

Marinate in *toyo* and *calamansi* juice with finely chopped garlic for a few hours in the refrigerator.

Cook the pork roll in the marinade and a little water till fork-tender. Cool and refrigerate so it will be easy to slice. Slice and wrap the roll in foil and bake at 350°F till nicely browned. Transfer to serving platter just before needed.

To make the gravy: Brown flour in butter, add the drippings and cream of mushroom and cook till done. Serve separately. Garnish roast with sliced button mushrooms or add this to the gravy. If you use *kalitiran* you don't have to roll the meat. Use it whole, as is.

Lengua Estofado

1 ox tongue or pork (upper portion of the
  pata)
Brown sugar
Vinegar
1 head garlic

Clean ox tongue by immersing in boiling water and scrape off outer layer.

Caramelize the brown sugar. Add vinegar and water and simmer till caramel is melted. Add pork or tongue, garlic and add water to cover. Boil and simmer till tender. (The garlic will taste like *butong pakwan*).

Cool and refrigerate till it can be sliced with ease. Serve with the thickened sauce in which pork or tongue was cooked.

Lengua Estofada

1 ox tongue
1 carrot
Leeks
Onion, whole
Peppercorns
Salt
1/2 cup butter
Pickle juice
Pickle relish
Garlic, generous amount, finely chopped
1 cup onion, finely chopped
Tomato sauce
Little sugar
Salt to taste
Pimiento, chopped

Prepare ox tongue as in previous recipe. Cook in water together with one carrot, leeks, whole onion, peppercorns, salt, till tender. Cool. Slice.

Sauté garlic and onion taking care not to brown it. Add the sliced tongue and broth, tomato sauce, pickle relish, pickle juice, little sugar and cook till sauce has thickened. Add pimiento; arrange on serving platter.

For the Chinese version of the *estofada*, just add *hibi*, *castañas* and dried mushrooms to the pork.

Going over my mother's recipe for Pork *Afritada* I realized she also cooked the liempo for her Dinuguan in a little water and browned it in its own fat. Her Sinigang na Karne and Asado de Carajay, on the other hand, were cooked in a mixture of tomatoes and onions till almost dry and browned in its own fat before the rest of the ingredients were thrown in.

Mother's Pork *Afritada*

1 kilo pork *kasim*
Garlic, onions, tomatoes
Salt to taste
Potatoes, peeled and quartered
Red and green peppers, seeded and sliced into
    strips

Cut pork into cubes. Cook in a little amount of water with some salt. Simmer until it's almost dry and oily. Lightly brown pork. Set pork aside and reduce the amount of oil in the skillet. Sauté the garlic, sliced onions and sliced tomatoes. Add the browned pork, add a little water and simmer till pork is almost tender. Add red and green pepper and remove from the heat.

If desired, you may fry the potatoes and add it when pork is tender, along with the peppers.

This recipe for Ham is from Azon, the late wife of my cousin Fidel. One of my readers told one of my cousins to let me know she swears by it, which is why I'm sharing it with you.

Azon's Ham

For every kilo of pork *pigue*:
10 tablespoons rock salt
8-9 tablespoons brown sugar
1 tablespoon *salitre*
1 1/2 cups water

Boil water and when it is boiling, add the salt and *salitre*. When these are dissolved, add the sugar. Remove from fire and cool.

Prick the meat deeply all over, rolling it in the solution while doing so.

Every day for the first week, prick the meat all over, rolling it in the solution and keeping it in the refrigerator for two weeks.

After two weeks, remove the meat from the solution and dry in strong sunlight for two days. Be sure to protect it from flies. Wrap it in tin foil and keep it in the freezer, the longer, the better, a week, a month, or more.

When it is to be cooked, boil the meat for one hour in medium heat in:

7 1/2 ounces pineapple juice
2/3 bottle beer
2 tablespoons brown sugar
1 bay leaf
A few peppercorns
A piece of cinnamon stick

When it's cooked, remove skin, cool, pack with brown sugar and "iron" it with red-hot steel.

Wrap in tin foil and store in freezer until needed.

My sister-in-law Puring has mastered her recipe for *Chicharon*, so much so that friends now keep their pork rind in the freezer and ask her to make it into *Chicharon* when they have collected a big batch.

Puring's Chicharon

Pig skin with layer of fat
Salt
Lard or cooking oil

Cut the pig skin into desired size. Wash and
drain well. Salt lightly. In a deep pan place the pig
skin in enough oil or lard to cover and bring to a boil.
Stir once in a while to prevent it from getting stuck to
each other. Reduce fire a little. As it cooks the texture
becomes soft and later it becomes firmer. At this point
take it out of the oil and let it cool. The next day heat
oil and deep fry until the skin crackles.

Keep precooked pork rind in airtight container
and deep fry only when needed.

One breakfast and lunchbox favorite is sausage or
longaniza. It's easy to prepare, doesn't spoil easily and
is always welcomed by kids. You can make your own
longaniza. Which is the more prudent thing to do, for
you will be in control of what goes into it.

You can be sure of the quality of the meat,
control the amount of fat used and do with little or no
nitrates. You can have them skinless or in casings as
you wish.

I remember my mother's version which consisted
of tiny cubed pork and a little fat cured with salt,

pepper and lots of slivered garlic.

Some of the *longaniza* recipes I'm sharing with you come from my only surviving aunt on my mother's side, a home economics teacher at Zamboanga Normal School (retired), Remedios Enrile.

Here are some points to remember when you make your own *longaniza*:

* Use quality meat—-fresh, with no unpleasant odor, discoloration, blood clots and unnecessary gristle.

* Use pork fat that is firm, taken from *pigue* or *kasim*.

* Use refined or table salt because it is concentrated and has the least amount of impurities as compared to rock salt.

* Use refined sugar rather than brown which caramelizes at a lower temperature and tends to darken the meat on cooking.

* Measure ingredients accurately. Too much sugar, for example, may result in acid formation which affects the color and palatability of the cured meat.

* Do not cure meats at room temperature for more than eight hours; refrigerate.

* Keep fat separate from the lean. Cut the fat into small cubes and grind the lean.

* Mix the ingredients by hand (wear plastic gloves), working with a kneading motion until the mixture becomes tacky.

* Place the mixture in a tray or basin and cover properly; cure in a refrigerator for the length of time specified for the type of sausage you're making.

Homemade *Longaniza*

1 1/2 kilos pork fat
3 kilos lean pork
1 cup vinegar
1 cup soy sauce
Salt to taste
1 large head garlic, pounded
Enough *pimiento* to color
Clean and dried pig's small intestines
1 1/2 tablespoons black pepper

Separate the fat from the lean meat of pork. Dice the pork fat into 1/2 centimeter cubes. Slice the meat into small pieces and chop fine. Add the other ingredients to mixture and mix thoroughly. Stuff in casings.

Spanish Sausage

2 pounds boneless lean pork, cut into large
    cubes or strips
1/2 pound fresh pork fat cut into cubes or
    strips
3/4 cup red wine vinegar
1 teaspoon oregano
3 cloves garlic, crushed
2 tablespoons salt
1 teaspoon paprika

1 teaspoon black pepper, cracked
1/2 teaspoon crushed red pepper
1/4 teaspoon sugar

Grind lean pork and fat together, using large hole disc of meat grinder. Add remaining ingredients. Mix thoroughly. Shape into patties, or roll for slicing or force mixture into casings.

Fresh Sausages

Pork fat, 1 part
Ground pork, lean, 2 parts
For every kilo of the above:
2 level tablespoons refined salt
1 1/2 level tablespoons refined sugar
1 1/2 tablespoons soy sauce
2 tablespoons *anisado* wine
1 level tablespoon chopped and fried garlic
1/2 level teaspoon *salitre*

Pass the lean pork through a meat grinder with 5/6-inch hole plate and cut the fat into small cubes. Place both in the same container and add the rest of ingredients. Mix the meat and other ingredients by hand until the mash becomes tacky, then cover the mixture with wax paper or plastic wrap and cure inside a refrigerator or cooler for five days.

After curing, stuff the mixture into casings and form into 2 or 3-inch long links. Store in the refrigerator or hang in a cool, clean, well-ventilated place until use.

Fresh Native Sausage

Cubed fat, 1 part
Ground or chopped lean meat, 2 parts
For every kilo, add:
2 1/2 tablespoons salt
2 1/2 level tablespoons sugar
1 1/2 level tablespoons soy sauce
2 tablespoons vinegar
2 tablespoons ground pepper
2 level teaspoons chopped garlic

Cure mixture in a cooler for 5-6 days and stuff into casings. Store in a cooler, ready for use.

To cook sausages:

Prick casings, add a little amount of water and cook in its own fat.

Poultry

❄❄❄❄

I came across a good piece of news for people like me who are concerned with their cholesterol level. It says that chicken skin contains only about 17% fat and that an equal portion of other meats has twice or thrice as much fat content.

Furthermore, two-thirds of the fat present is unsaturated. Still the advice is, if you're really counting calories, don't eat the skin. It's best to remove the skin before cooking the chicken. I used to save all my chicken skin in the freezer for a granddaughter who loves chicken skin cracklings.

Luckily for her health and her ballet partner, she got tired of it and all my chicken skin now goes to waste. Today, chicken is probably the cheapest meat available in the market. You can buy it freshly slaughtered in wet markets, whole or cut up--- drumsticks, thighs, breasts, soup bones, liver and gizzards, heads, wings, and feet. It is also available, whole or cut up, frozen, in supermarkets. Seasoned chicken ready for cooking is also available in various brands.

All this is a far cry from the days when we had to buy our chickens live, then slaughter and dress them ourselves. As a teenager, I learned how to kill a chicken—stepping on the wings held together with a foot to keep them from flapping, getting hold of the head with the left hand and slashing the throat with a sharp knife with the right hand.

My mother also taught me to save the chicken blood for our *dinuguan*. She never trusted the quality of pig's blood sold in the wet markets.

How often have you heard the advice: "Learn to use herbs instead of salt in your cooking; it's healthier"?

Some of the chicken recipes that follow are flavored with herbs—lemon grass, *cilantro*, dill, mint, chives—and call for no salt at all.

Healthy and flavorful cooking indeed!

Roasted Chicken with Lemon Grass

1 roasting chicken, about 2 kilos
10 lemon grass stalks, thinly sliced
1 small whole lemon, rind pierced with a
     fork
1 1/2 cups fresh *cilantro* sprigs
1/2 cup finely minced fresh *cilantro*
2 tablespoons minced lemon zest
Freshly ground pepper
2 cups chicken broth
14 garlic cloves, peeled

Preheat oven to 350°F . Rinse the chicken well inside out and pat dry. Sprinkle the cavity with 1 thinly sliced lemon grass stalk. Place the whole lemon in the cavity. Arrange the *cilantro* sprigs around the lemon and tie the chicken's legs together. In a small bowl, mix the remaining sliced lemon grass, 1/4 cup minced *cilantro* and lemon zest. Gently lift the skin, being careful not to tear it, from the neck end of the chicken and spread the lemon grass mixture over the flesh.

Place the chicken in a roasting pan and season with the ground pepper. Pour in chicken broth and scatter the garlic and remaining minced *cilantro* in the roasting pan. Place the chicken in the oven. Roast for 2 to 2 1/2 hours, basting every 15 minutes.

A Honey of a Hen

1 whole chicken, about 1 kilo
2 lemons, thinly sliced
1 packed cup fresh mint leaves
4 tablespoons honey
2 tablespoons fresh lemon juice

Preheat oven to 400°F. Rinse the chicken inside out and pat dry. Place the chicken upside down on work surface. With your fingers, gently separate the skin from the flesh, being careful not to tear skin. Insert one lemon slice on each side of the back bone. Truss the opening with a metal skewer. Turn the bird over. Carefully loosen the skin from the breast, legs and thighs. Insert slices of lemon to cover as much flesh as possible. Place the remaining lemon slices and mint in the cavity and truss with a metal skewer. Place the chicken on a rack in a foil-lined baking pan.

Combine the honey and lemon juice. Place the chicken in the oven. Cook for 1 to 1-1/2 hours, basting with the honey-lemon mixture every 10 minutes, or until the juice runs clear when the thigh is pierced with a fork. Cut into serving pieces; discard the lemon and mint. Serve immediately.

Chicken Stew

2 boneless, skinless chicken breasts
2 garlic cloves, minced
1 cup minced fresh chives
1/2 cup dill, minced
1/8 teaspoon ground nutmeg
1 1/2 cups peeled baby carrots
1 1/2 cups coarsely chopped onion
1 1/2 cups chicken broth
2 cups sugar snap peas (or substitute)
1 cup low-fat blend (recipe follows)
Freshly ground pepper

In a large stockpot, place the chicken, garlic, 1/2 cup dill, hives, nutmeg, carrots, onion and chicken broth. Bring to a boil, reduce the heat and simmer, covered, for 20 minutes or until carrots are tender. Add the peas and simmer for 10 minutes, until peas are tender. Add the remaining dill, low-fat blend, and pepper to taste.

Serve warm.

Low-Fat Blend: Place 1 cup non-fat plain yogurt and 1 cup low-fat or non-fat cottage cheese in a blender and blend until smooth. Makes 2 cups. Refrigerate 1 cup for future use.

Everyday Garlic Chicken

1 whole chicken, about 1 1/2 kilos
2 teaspoons ground ginger
1 whole lemon, pricked several times
24 garlic cloves, peeled
3 cups chicken broth
Freshly ground pepper

Pre-heat oven to 400°F.

Rinse the chicken and pat it dry inside and out. Place the lemon in the cavity and place the chicken in a small roasting pan. Cut 1 clove of garlic in half and rub over the breast skin. Place the chicken in the oven and bake for 20 minutes; add 1-1/2 cups of broth and bake for another 20 minutes.   Reduce the heat to 375°F, add the remaining broth and garlic, and cook for 30 to 40 minutes, basting every 10 to 15 minutes.

Remove the chicken from the pan and place it on platter, breast side down, to rest for 10 to 15 minutes.

Pour the collected juices into a fat-skimming cup and de-fat. With a fork, mash the garlic. Place the garlic and de-fatted juices back in the roasting pan. Over medium-high heat, reduce the liquid by half, stirring frequently. Strain if you desire a smooth sauce. Carve the chicken and pass the sauce at the table.

One of my friends has always maintained that "the closer to the bone, the sweeter the meat." Anyone who has feasted on chicken wings knows how true this is. My boss one time looked down on a serving plate of chicken wings, but when she had tried some, she instantly became a chicken wings convert.

So if you've been staying away from chicken wings because there's not much meat, find out what you have been missing by trying them.

Fried, broiled or baked, they can serve as appetizers or as one of the main dish offerings.

Sweet-Sour Wings

1 1/2 kilos broiler-fryer chicken wings
1 teaspoon salt
Vegetable oil for browning
1 cup cornstarch
3 eggs, beaten
1/4 cup soy sauce
1/2 cup vinegar
1/2 cup sugar

3 tablespoons ketchup
1/2 teaspoon salt
1/2 cup red currant jelly
2 tablespoons lemon juice

Season chicken wings with salt. Mix cornstarch and eggs and dip chicken wings to coat. Deep fry till golden. Drain.

Mix the rest of the ingredients and cook for 10 minutes. Place fried chicken wings in shallow pan. Pour glaze over chicken and bake at 350°F for 30 minutes or until glazed. Turn for even glaze.

This *Estofado de Manok* is a family favorite of the Tarrozas of Zamboanga City. They refer to it as "*Punta'y Dedo*" because no one can make it like their Grandma Inez. "*Ni punta'y dedo*," they say of other versions. "*Wala sa kalingkingan*," as the Tagalogs say.

Estofado de Manok (Punta'y Dedo)

1 broiler chicken, cut up
Marinade:
    Calamansi or vinegar
    Toyo

Pepper
Garlic
Pinch of sugar
Salt
Potatoes, quartered
Carrots, cut into chunks
Bell pepper, sliced
Chorizo bilbao, sliced
Cheese, grated
Butter
1 small can liver spread
1 tetrapak tomato sauce
Sweet peas
Olives
Raisins

Marinate the chicken in the *calamansi* or vinegar, *toyo*, pepper, garlic, pinch of sugar and salt.

Half cook the chicken in small amount of oil. Set aside.

Fry potatoes, carrots and bell pepper and set aside.

Cook chicken in the marinade together with the *chorizo bilbao*, grated cheese, little butter, the liver spread and tomato sauce. Cook till tender.

Add fried vegetables, raisins, olives and peas.

(One of the Tarroza girls says she adds cornstarch dissolved in a little water if the sauce is too thin.)

Pork/Chicken/ Liver a la Inez

1 kilo *lomo*/liver/chicken
Calamansi or vinegar
Garlic
Pepper
Toyo
Ketchup
Onion rings

Cook the *lomo* or liver or chicken in the rest of the ingredients except onion rings adobo style. When almost done add about 3 cooking laddlespoons of ketchup. Stir while cooking. Just before removing from the fire, add onion rings and stir- fry crisp. Serve hot.

The Chicken with Lambanog is a very simple family recipe from Elayda Marasigan who comes from the Caballes family of Pagsanjan, Laguna. The sweet-sour braised Chicken recipe is my mother's; the Chicken in Liver Sauce, my cousin Med's.

Chicken with *Lambanog*

1 broiler chicken
Clarified butter
1 onion, minced
4 tablespoons *lambanog*
Salt
Pepper
Potatoes, quartered
Sweetpeas (optional)

Cut chicken into serving pieces. Sauté onion in clarified butter. Add chicken and sauté till lightly brown. Add the *lambanog* and season to taste with salt and pepper. Simmer till almost tender. Add the potatoes and cook in slow fire till done.

Chicken in Liver Sauce

1 broiler chicken, cut into serving pieces
Flour
Cornstarch
Cooking oil
Chicken liver
Salt
Pepper
Butter
Chopped onion

Broil chicken liver and pound fine. Set aside.
Dredge chicken with flour-cornstarch mixture. Lightly brown chicken in oil.

Sauté chopped onion in butter. Add chicken and seasonings and cook over low fire till almost tender. Add liver and simmer till chicken is tender and sauce is thick.

Tinolang Manok with Tanglad

2 tablespoons cooking oil
Garlic, crushed
1 onion, sliced
Piece of ginger, peeled and sliced
1 chicken, cut into serving pieces
2 tablespoons patis
Salt to taste
Pinch of pepper
5 cups rice washing
1 gizzard
1 green papaya, pared and cubed
5 pieces tanglad leaves
Bunch of sili leaves

Sauté garlic, onion, ginger, gizzard, and chicken. Season with patis, salt and pepper. Add rice washing and bring to a boil.

Simmer for 15 minutes. Add green papaya

and *tanglad* and cook for 10 minutes. Add *sili* leaves and cook for another minute. Serve hot.

Huli-Huli Chicken

3 broiler-fryers
Marinade:
1/4 cup ketchup
1/4 cup soy sauce
1/2 cup white wine or chicken broth
3 tablespoons frozen concentrate of pineapple
    juice
1 tablespoon finely chopped ginger

Soak chicken in marinade. Grill, brushing occasionally with marinade.

Crispy Chicken Nuggets

1/2 kilo skinned and boned chicken breasts,
    trimmed of all fat and cut in 2 1/4-inch
    as long by 1-inch wide pieces
White from 1 large egg
2/3 cup seasoned breadcrumbs mixed with 1
    teaspoon Creole, Mexican or Italian
    seasoning

Whisk egg white in a large bowl until foamy. Add chicken and mix gently to coat. Spread about half the crumb mixture on waxed paper. Lay half the chicken pieces on top and turn each piece once to coat with a thin layer of crumbs. Place in a single layer on large plate. Repeat with remaining crumb mixture and chicken. Cover with plastic wrap and refrigerate until ready to bake—up to 24 hours. Heat oven to 450°F. Line a baking sheet with foil. Lightly coat with vegetable shortening. Arrange chicken in single layer on foil, then lightly spray with cooking spray. Bake for 15 minutes or until chicken is golden and opaque in the middle. Serve hot. Makes 36 pieces.

Fried chicken is a great favorite for picnics, packed lunches, parties or everyday meals. One reason for its versatility, perhaps, is it is equally good hot or cold.

Every cook probably has his own method for a crisp, delicate and tender chicken. My cousin's cook, for example, does not cover the skillet while frying the chicken. The orthodox way, I think.

I have my own method, however, which works fine for me. I start with hot oil but turn the heat to medium-low and keep the lid on during the early stage of frying. (I like my fried chicken cooked thoroughly). To brown the chicken and crisp the skin I take off the lid and turn on the heat higher during the latter part of cooking time.

Make sure your oil is hot before adding the chicken

pieces. Nothing spoils one's appetite for fried chicken than greasy and heavy chicken.

Batter-Fried Chicken

1 broiler-fryer, cut into serving pieces
1/2 cup all-purpose flour
Salad oil for frying

Batter:
1 1/2 cups all-purpose flour, sifted
2 teaspoons baking powder
2 teaspoons salt
1/4 teaspoon pepper
2 eggs
3/4 cup milk
1 1/2 tablespoons salad oil

Wipe chicken well with damp paper towels. Roll in flour.

In deep-fat fryer or deep skillet, slowly heat oil (at least 2 inches deep) to 350°F on deep-frying thermometer. Also, preheat oven to 300°F.

Meanwhile, make batter: Sift flour with baking powder, salt and pepper; set aside. In medium bowl with rotary beater beat eggs, milk and oil until combined. Add flour mixture gradually, beating until smooth.

Dip floured chicken pieces in batter to coat evenly. Deep-fry a few pieces at a time and turning several times, 18 to 20 minutes, or until brown and tender. Drain well on paper towels.

Place cooked chicken in shallow pan in oven to keep warm while rest of chicken cooks.

For curried fried chicken, add 3 teaspoons curry powder to ingredients before coating chicken pieces.

You can serve batter-fried chicken with the following sauce:

2 cups canned tomato puree
1 clove garlic, finely chopped
1 can pimientos, drained and cut into strips
1 1/2 teaspoons salt
Dash of pepper

Combine all sauce ingredients. Simmer, covered, for 30 minutes. Spoon sauce over chicken.

Other flavor varieties: Roll chicken in mixture of 1/2 cup grated Parmesan cheese, 1 1/2 teaspoons salt, 1 teaspoon dried oregano leaves, 1/4 teaspoon pepper and 1 teaspoon paprika.

Oven-Fried Chicken

1 broiler-fryer, cut into serving pieces
1/2 cup all-purpose flour
1 teaspoon salt
1/2 teaspoon pepper

1/2 teaspoon poultry seasoning
1/2 cup melted butter/margarine

Preheat oven to 400°F.

Pat chicken pieces with damp paper towel.

In a clean paper bag combine flour, salt, pepper and poultry seasoning. Shake chicken in bag, a few pieces at a time, coating well.

Arrange chicken in a very shallow pan such as a 15" x 10" x 2" pan. Brush butter or margarine over chicken. Cover pan with foil. Bake 30 minutes. Remove foil. Increase oven temperature to 450°F, bake 15 to 20 minutes more or till fork-tender and golden brown.

Quick Roast Chicken

1 regular-sized chicken
1 tablespoon salt
1 tablespoon lard
1 onion
Peppercorns
3 pieces *calamansi*
1 clean, empty can of biscuit opened at one
    end
1 1/2-foot-long stick made of bamboo, wood
    or iron

Hang the chicken to allow liquid to drain. Rub salt and *calamansi* juice all over the chicken before cooking. Chop the onions, mix the salt, pepper and the rest of the ingredients and seal cavity with needle and thread.

Skewer the chicken on the stick and choosing a clean spot, stick the skewered chicken firmly into the ground and invert the biscuit can over the chicken. Build a fire around the can and keep it burning from 15 to 20 minutes to cook the chicken to a juicy golden brown.

Roast Chicken Stuffed with Curried Rice

1 roasting chicken, whole
***Toyo* and *calamansi* for marinating**
Cooked rice
Butter
Garlic
Curry powder

Marinate the chicken in *toyo* and *calamansi* for at least 30 minutes.

In the meantime, in a skillet, melt the butter and sauté the garlic and curry powder. Add the cooked rice and cook a little longer until well-blended. Remove the chicken from the marinade and stuff, really stuff, the chicken with the curried rice. Secure openings. Wrap the chicken tightly in foil and bake in a roaster pan at 350°F for about an hour. About 15 minutes before cooking time is up, open the foil wrapper carefully to expose the chicken so it will brown nicely. Be careful not to burn your face or hands in the steam that is trapped in the foil packet.

To serve: Carefully carve the chicken into serving pieces and mound the rice in the middle of serving platter. Arrange the chicken pieces around the rice.

Fish
&
Seafood

❄❄❄❄

Good news for cholesterol-conscious folks is an item I read that says today's better analysis methods reveal that mollusks such as clams, oysters and scallops have actually less cholesterol than beef.

And that though shrimp, lobster and crab contain more cholesterol we need not cut them out of our diets entirely, only eat them less often.

Good sources of Omega-3, the report says, are salmon, mackerel, trout, tuna, shrimp and crab. As you probably have heard, Omega-3, which is found in sea animals, may help reduce the risk of heart disease.

A few tips on handling fish:

Broiling
* Sprinkle fish with salt and pepper, brush with lemon juice and melted butter, margarine or oil and broil until fish is golden and flesh is flaky when forked.
* Fillets and small pieces of fish can be broiled on the side. There is no need to turn fish to prevent drying,

Pan-frying or sautéing
* Rub with lemon or lime juice and season with salt and pepper. Dip in flour, then in beaten egg with 1/2 cup milk, and finally in breadcrumbs. Pan fry in butter or margarine in large skillet. Cook 5 minutes or more until golden brown and crusty and the flesh is tender and flaky.
* Cook only a few pieces at a time and do not overcrowd pan.

Shallow deep-fat frying

* You need only enough oil to cover fish 3/4 to
1 inch deep. Leave at least 1 inch of space to top of
frying pan to avoid boiling over.

* Heat oil but do not wait for it to smoke; that
will be too hot and fish will brown before it's cooked.

* Brown on one side, turn to cook on the other.
Drain.

Poaching

* This method can be used for fillets or whole fish
and can be done in the oven or top of the range.

* Liquid may be wine, salted water or milk. Or
a combination of white wine, thinly sliced onion rings,
parlsey, slivered garlic, bay leaves and celery.

Baking

* This is best for large, stuffed, whole fish.

* Use a hot oven 400°F to 425°F.

* Bake fish in a large shallow well-greased pan.

* A little stock of wine in the pan will steam
slightly and prevent it from drying out. Baste once in
a while with liquid at bottom of pan.

The next three fish recipes are from a collection of
Spanish recipes lent to me by Leticia Valeriano who
was in the same cooking class I was in many years ago.

I painstakingly translated them from Spanish to
English with the help of a dictionary, my three units of

Spanish in college and my knowledge of Chabacano (pidgin Spanish spoken in Zamboanga City).

Pastel de Pescado

1 fish (white meat)
2 potatoes
1 carrot
1 onion
Mushrooms

Scale and clean fish. Debone and cut into cubes. Peel and cut potatoes and carrots into cubes. Slice onions.

Fry potatoes, carrots, onions, mushrooms and fish. Add fish stock. Cook. Place in a deep pie plate. Cover with crust and bake in a moderate oven until crust is ligthly brown.

To make crust:

2 cups flour
1/2 teaspoon salt
4 tablespoons butter
2 egg yolks
Ice water

Mix dry ingredients, make a hole in center of pile and add the butter, egg yolks and work with fingers till crumbly. Add enough water to make a dough neither too dry nor too wet. Roll out and cover fish in pie plate. Bake.

Pescado a la Jardinera

Fish, white meat
1 onion, sliced in rings
1 laurel leaf
1/2 can asparagus
2 tablespoons oil
2 tomatoes
Pechay
Green onions
Cabbage leaves
Salt to taste
1 1/2 cups fish stock
Sweet garden peas

Arrange the vegetables except the sweet peas in baking plate. Top with fish. Add salt to taste and pour in stock. Bake in moderate oven until fish is cooked. Thicken the sauce with 2 tablespoons flour, 3 tablespoons butter. Add peas.

Pescado a la Matelot

Fish (*apahap*, *lapu-lapu* or *talakitok*)
1/2 onion
1/2 cup Jerez
1 cup soup stock
1 laurel leaf
Salt to taste

Clean fish. Salt it. Place in a baking dish together with the rest of the ingredients. Bake in a moderate oven till cooked.

Serve with this sauce:

4 tablespoons butter
3 tablespoons flour
1 cup milk
1 cup fish broth
1 tablespoon chopped parsley
1 can mushrooms

Melt the butter in a small saucepan. Brown the flour. Gradually add fish stock and milk and cook till smooth.

Pour over baked fish and garnish with parsley and mushrooms.

After ascertaining that I eat *hito*, my friend Emy Inocencio sent me 2 big *hito* on my birthday. She had it cleaned and all I had to do was cook it.

Along with the *hito* of Taiwan variety which is farm raised, she sent me a couple of *hito* recipes.

To clean hito:

* Put the live hito in a plastic container, sprinkle with some salt, cover, and it will be all over for the hito in a little while.

* Pull out the gills and intestines through the head.

* Behind the head you will find something like earlobes. Make slits on both sides of the head and remove that tiny brown portion which is the liver.

* Rub the skin with salt to remove the sliminess.

* If you have wood ash, you may want to scrub the *hito* with it to whiten the skin.

Adobong Hito sa Gata

Hito, cut into serving pieces
Tanglad (lemon grass)
Onion
Salt
Vinegar
Ginger
Coconut milk (first extraction)

Line a *carajay* with *tanglad* leaves. Place the *hito* on top. Add the onion, ginger, salt to taste, vinegar. When it's almost cooked, add the coconut milk and let boil for another 10 minutes or till coconut milk is very thick.

Adobong Hito

Cook *hito* just like ordinary *adobo*. Add lard when it's cooked.

Charcoal-Broiled *Hito*

Broil whole fish over charcoal fire. Brush with *calamansi* juice mixed with vegetable oil or corn oil to prevent drying. Serve with juice from boiled tamarind and *bagoong*.

Tochong Hito

Hito, cut into serving pieces
Garlic, crushed
Onion, sliced
Ginger, sliced
Tomatoes, sliced
Vinegar
Tahure
Ampalaya
Eggplant
Rice washing
Sugar (optional)

Fry the *hito*. Set aside. Sauté garlic, sliced onion, ginger and tomatoes. Add *tahure* mixed with rice washing and vinegar. Let boil. Add cut-up eggplant and *ampalaya*. Add the fried *hito* last. Season to taste.

Sinigang na Hito sa Miso

Hito, cut into serving pieces
Garlic
Onion
Ginger
Tomatoes
Miso
Rice washing
Tamarind
Mustasa leaves
Pepper

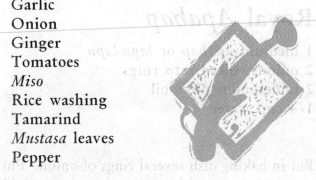

Sauté garlic, sliced onion, ginger and tomatoes. Add *miso* and sauté. Add rice washing and let boil. Add *hito*. When it's cooked add the *mustasa* leaves and pepper. Season with *patis* to taste.

Chicharong Hito

Boil *hito* in water with *tanglad* and salt for a few minutes till soft. Flake flesh and fry in hot oil till crisp. Serve with tamarind extract mixed with *patis* and chili sauce.

Royal *Apahap*

1 medium *apahap* or *lapu-lapu*
2 onions, sliced into rings
2 tablespoons olive oil
1/4 cup water

Put in baking dish several rings of onion. Put the fish on top and top with more onion rings. Add the olive oil and water. Bake in moderate oven (350°F) for 20 minutes.
Sauce:
2 cloves garlic, crushed
1 small onion, minced
1 cup tomato sauce
1 cup mayonnaise

Meantime, sauté the garlic, onion and tomato sauce. Simmer for 15 minutes. Pour over the fish and bake fish for 20 minutes. Cover top of fish with mayonnaise and put back in oven for 5 to 10 minutes. Serve hot.

On a day I spent at the beach in Lemery, Batangas, our host, in response to our inquiry on how their *sinaing* is prepared, insisted on preparing one small *palayok* of *sinaing* for each of us in our party. How's that for Filipino hospitality?

Sinaing na Tulingan

Tulingan
Dried *kamias*
Salt

Prepare the fish removing the gills and internal organs. Wash well. Make about two diagonal slits on each side of the fish and flatten fish with your fingers. Salt fish.

Arrange fish in layers in *palayok* with dried *kamias* between layers, add enough water to cover. Bring to a boil and reduce fire to cook slowly until the water has been reduced to a minimum. The spines will be soft but the flesh firm. Good with garlic rice and tomatoes.

This very simple but tasty dish is shared by my cousin Nenggay of Zamboanga City. Perhaps the secret is in the freshness of the fish.

Buro

1 kilo fish (*caballas* in *chabacano*, *hasa-hasa* to *Tagalogs*)
Salt
6 cups coconut milk
Salt and pepper to taste

Use very fresh fish. Split the fish lengthwise. Salt it generously and let stand for half an hour. Sun-dry for 2 to 3 days. Wash the fish well to remove the excess salt. Cook in coconut milk until it becomes oily, turning occasionally.

If the only way you cook your *tilapia* is by frying or broiling it, you'll be surprised at the many ways Visayan women prepare the fish. They not only use the more familiar *gabi* leaves for wrapping the fish but also *pechay* leaves. They stuff it with a mixture of tomatoes, onion and ginger like we do with our *bangus*. Many of their *tilapia* recipes also make use of coconut milk and when cooked with different vegetables make a one-dish meal.

The recipes here were among the entries to a *tilapia* cooking contest held in Iloilo City by the Bureau of Fisheries and Aquatic Resources (BFAR) in 1979.

Berry Pelaez-Marfori, whose husband raises tilapia, says she hands out xeroxed copies of these tilapia recipes that appeared in *Kusina* to her husband's customers.

Broiled *Tilapia* (Aklan)

1 piece *tilapia*
1 onion, chopped
1 *calamansi*
1 tomato, chopped
1/8 teaspoon pepper
1 teaspoon oil
Salt to taste

Clean the fish and slit the belly. Stuff with mixture of tomatoes, onion and salt to taste. Rub fish with *calamansi* juice and oil. Wrap in aluminum foil and broil.

Adobong Tilapia (Roxas City)

6 pieces *tilapia*
2 tablespoons oil
4 cloves garlic, crushed
Black peppercorns
1/2 cup vinegar
Bay leaf
2 tablespoons soy sauce
Salt to taste

Clean the fish (scale it too). Place fish in a saucepan and add the rest of the ingredients. Cook over medium fire until fish is done.

Pinangat na Tilapia (Iloilo)

1/2 kilo *tilapia*
1 onion, chopped
1 small piece ginger, pared and minced
2 cups thick coconut milk
10 pieces tomatoes, sliced
Salt to taste
Achuete for coloring
Gabi leaves

Clean and scale *tilapia*. Set aside. Mix tomatoes, onion and ginger and season with salt. Marinate *tilapia* in this mixture for 10 to 15 minutes. Wrap *tilapia* together with mixture in gabi leaves. Arrange in a saucepan and add coconut milk. Add a little water. Season with salt. Boil and cook until coconut milk is thick. Serve hot.

Pinaksiwang Tilapia

6 pieces *tilapia*
1 cup coconut milk
1/2 cup vinegar
Piece of ginger
Sliced guava leaves
Salt to taste

Clean fish and scale it. Wash thoroughly. Place fish in a saucepan and add all the ingredients. Let boil and cook until fish is done.

Tilapia Paksiw (Bacolod)

6 pieces fish
1 medium-size onion, sliced
1 piece ginger, sliced
5 pieces *okra*, sliced
2 pieces sweet pepper, sliced

1/2 cup vinegar
5 cloves garlic, minced
1/4 teaspoon soy sauce
5 pieces string beans

Clean and scale fish. Arrange fish and rest of the ingredients in a saucepan. Add salt to taste. Cover and cook for 10 to 15 minutes.

Tilapiang Ginataan
(Negros Occidental)

6 pieces *tilapia*
2 cups coconut milk
1 cup vinegar
3 cloves garlic, minced
1/4 cup onion, sliced
1 piece red pepper, sliced
1 piece green pepper, sliced
1 piece ginger, sliced
1 piece eggplant, sliced
1/2 cup squash, sliced
1 piece *ampalaya*, sliced
Salt to taste

Clean fish. Place in a saucepan. Add vinegar, salt, coconut milk, garlic and ginger. Boil for 5 minutes.

Add squash and eggplant and cook until almost done.
Add onions, red and green pepper and *ampalaya*. Add
salt to taste. Cook until vegetables are done.

Tilapia Salad (Iloilo)

5 pieces medium-size *tilapia*
5 pieces sweet potatoes
1 piece carrot
5 pieces string beans, cut into 2-inch lengths
1 cup mayonnaise
1 hard-boiled egg
1 piece onion
1 can sliced pineapple

Boil sweet potatoes and carrot. Cut in cubes.
Steam *tilapia* and flake. Chop onion and mash egg.
Combine all ingredients. Season with salt and pepper
to taste. Chill for 10 to 15 minutes. Serve cold.

If you haven't yet discovered the joy of cooking with
tanglad (lemon grass), it's about time you did. *Tanglad*
imparts a strong lemon-like aroma and flavor and is a
good source of Vitamin A.

You can use it in your *paksiw*, *sinigang*, *nilaga*,
adobo, and *guinatan* of vegetables or chicken.

To grow *tanglad* successfully, be sure it gets plenty of sunshine. Take care when handling the leaves, which are rather sharp and can cause tiny cuts in the skin.

These recipes come from a book on alternate food produced by the Food Science and Nutrition Department of UP, and a collection of herbal recipes by Erlinda Castro Sanqui, who developed the now widely used *Pito-pito*.

Shrimps with *Tanglad* Leaves

1 cup pure coconut milk
2 cups coconut milk, second extraction
2 tablespoons salt
3/4 cup shrimp, whole
5 pieces *tanglad* leaves
3 *cucharita* leaves

Extract pure coconut milk from grated coconut. Set aside. Add 1-1/2 cups hot water to grated coconut for second extraction. Season with salt. Add shrimp. Cook for 10 minutes. Add *tanglad* and let boil. Add *cucharita* leaves and cook for 2 minutes. Add pure coconut milk, constantly stirring to avoid curdling. Cook for 1 minute.

Sinigang na Isda with *Tanglad*

4 cups rice washing
1 onion, sliced
8 pieces *kamias*
6 slices *bangus*
1 1/2 tablespoons salt
5 pieces *tanglad*
1 pack *sitaw*, cut up
1 pack *sigarilyas*
1 pack *kangkong*

Boil water with onion and *kamias*. Add fish, salt and *tanglad*. Add *sitaw* and *sigarilyas*. When nearly done, add *kangkong* and simmer for 2 minutes. Serve hot.

Fish with *Tanglad* and Coconut Milk

1/2 kilo fish, scaled and cleaned
1 cup coconut milk
2 stalks *tanglad*, cut into 4 pieces
1/4 cup pure coco vinegar
Salt to taste

1 hot pepper for aroma
1 medium onion, sliced thinly

In a cooking pot arrange *tanglad*, fish, hot pepper and onion. Add vinegar, salt and coconut milk. Bring to a boil. Lower heat and cook 15 minutes.

Fish in Herb and Coconut Milk Sauce

8 medium *tilapia*, cleaned
2 cups coconut milk
2 cups *kangkong*, chopped
8 pieces *gabi* leaves
3 small chilies, crushed
7 strands *tanglad*, cut up into 4 equal parts
1 tablespoon ginger, crushed
Salt to taste
2 cloves garlic, minced

Wrap *tilapia* individually in gabi leaves. Line cooking pot with *tanglad* leaves. Arrange *tilapia* in cooking pot. On top arrange chopped *kangkong*, chilies, garlic and onion. Pour coconut milk, add salt. Cook over low heat for 15 minutes.

Dinimdiman (Pangasinan) and *Ugadaan* (La Union) are from Sonia de Leon's collection of non-traditional foods compiled in the course of a nationwide study she made with a team of University of the Philippines home economists.

Dinimdiman (Pangasinan)

Pating
Coconut milk
Sugar
Peppercorns
Onion
Garlic
Vinegar
Salt
Water

Clean fish and cut into serving pieces. Cook fish with garlic, onion, vinegar, salt and peppercorns. When fish is tender add sugar and coconut milk; season to taste and cook till done.

Ugadaan (La Union)

Pagi (sting ray)
Coconut milk
Tomatoes, thinly sliced
Onion, sliced
Garlic, crushed
Achuete water
Oil
Salt to taste

Clean *pagi* and cut into serving pieces. Heat oil
and sauté garlic, onion and tomatoes. Stir in *achuete*
water. Add *pagi* and season with salt. Simmer until
pagi is tender. Add coconut milk, stir and allow to boil
before removing from fire.

Mussels, locally known as *tahong*, are a rich source of
calcium and protein and a great delicacy, too. Whoever
called them the "oysters of the poor" didn't know what
he was talking about. We should feast on them on red-
tide-free days.

I remember on one trip to Poro Point in La
Union we cooked a big batch of *tahong* over a coal fire
and the juicy and succulent tidbits never got to the
dining table.

But innovative cooks have devised more ways of
serving mussels. These are recipes of Ramon A. Obusan

and Erodina E. Urbano. I got them from fellow Soroptimist Amadea Medina who until her retirement was chief of the Home Economics Division of the Bureau of Agricultural Extension (BAE).

Mussels deteriorate rapidly so how can one tell which is fresh?

* Open or cracked shells indicate mussels are dead.

* If slightly open, live shell will close tightly when tapped.

* Best are tightly-closed shells that are moist, intact and not chipped.

* Slice the two halves of the shell across each other; if they budge, the shell is probably filled with mud. Discard.

To clean:
* Scrub with stiff brush under cold water.
* Pull off the beard visible between shells.
* Remove the beard just before cooking—mussels will die once they are debearded.

Rellenong Tahong

2 cups *tahong*, cooked, removed from shell, and
  chopped
1 small box raisins
1 large potato, cooked and mashed
1 onion, sliced
2 eggs, beaten

1/2 cup ground *biskotso*
2 cups oil
30 pieces large *tahong* shells, cleaned

Mix first four ingredients well. Season with salt.
Add *biskotso* to beaten egg.

Spoon some *tahong* mixture into each *tahong* half
shell. Pour or dip each filled shell into egg mixture and
fry in deep fat. Serve with *ketchup*.

Tortang Tahong

1 cup *tahong*, cooked and removed from shell
1/2 small box of raisins
Sweet peas, cooked, drained
1 potato, cubed
3 cloves garlic, crushed
1 onion, sliced
1 large tomato, sliced
4 eggs, beaten
1/2 cup oil
Salt to taste

Sauté garlic, onion, tomato and add *tahong*,
potatoes, peas and raisins. Stir once in a while. Cool
when cooked.

Heat a non-stick skillet, add a little oil and pour
in the beaten egg, spreading it thinly in the skillet.

Add the *tahong* mixture on one half and flip over the other half of the egg. Serve with ketchup.

Tahong Q

150 pieces large *tahong*
1 head garlic
3 1/2 cups vinegar
1/2 cup soy sauce
1 teaspoon ground pepper
50 barbecue sticks

Steam the *tahong*; remove from shells. Drain and marinate in mixture of vinegar, soy sauce, salt and pepper at least one hour. Drain. Skewer three pieces of *tahong* per barbecue stick. Deep-fry each *tahong* stick. Serve hot or cold with a vinegar-garlic dip.

Adobong Tahong

2 cups *tahong*, cooked and removed from shell
1 onion, sliced
5 cloves garlic
1 cup vinegar
1/2 teaspoon ground pepper
2 tablespoons soy sauce

Cook vinegar, soy sauce, garlic and onion. When mixture boils, add the *tahong* and cook for 2 minutes. Season with salt and pepper. Serve hot.

Tahong with Pineapple

3 cups *tahong*, steamed and removed from shell
3 cloves garlic
1 onion, sliced
3 tomatoes, sliced
1 can pineapple chunks, drained
2 to 3 tablespoons vinegar

Sauté the garlic, onion and tomatoes. Add vinegar to drained pineapple chunks and cook for 2 minutes. Add to *tahong* and tomato mixture. Check seasoning. Serve hot or cold.

Mussels *Bicolandia*

2 cups parboiled mussels meat
10 pieces blanched *pechay* leaves
2 teaspoons chopped ginger
1 medium tomato, chopped
1 medium onion, chopped
1/4 cup coconut milk

1 1/4 cups cococream
Salt

Season mussels with ginger and salt. Mix together with tomatoes and onion.

Wring *pechay* leaves to get rid of excess liquid. Take care not to tear them. Spread and separate the leaves.

Get a leaf and place 4 to 5 mussels in the center, top with a heaping teaspoon of the tomato-onion mixture, season with salt; spoon 1 teaspoon cococream on top. Then wrap by folding the leaf securely over the filling. Do the same with the rest of the ingredients.

Place stuffed leaves, peppers and cocomilk in a pan and let simmer, covered, for 30 to 45 minutes. Turn over stuffed leaves gently after first half of cooking. Check seasoning.

Add remaining cococream and let cook for a minute before serving.

The Stuffed *Adobong Pusit* is really good. It is a regular in cook Leonora Lopez' repertoire of recipes she learned from the families she has served, among them the Olondriz, Bayot and Carpo families.

To clean squid:

* Pull out head from the body taking care not to pierce the ink sac.

* Pull out the cartillage attached to the body. In

a smaller squid, this cartillage is discarded. In the cuttlefish this cartillage is boiled and dried and used in bird cages.

* Remove the squid's teeth—the round mass found at the base of the head.

* Remove and discard the yellowish pouch and attached membranes.

* Carefully separate the ink sac and set aside.

* Remove the thin covering on the body and rinse well under running water.

* Use as directed.

Stuffed Squid

6 medium-size squid
1 teaspoon vinegar
1/4 teaspoon salt
1/4 cup water
2 tablespoons cooking oil
1/2 teaspoon garlic, minced
1/4 cup onion, chopped
1/4 cup tomatoes, chopped
1/2 cup shrimp, chopped
Little sugar
1/4 cup celery, chopped
1/4 teaspoon Worcestershire sauce
1/4 teaspoon vinegar
1/2 teaspoon salt

Dash of pepper
Oil for frying

Prepare the squid. Remove tentacles and set aside. Cook bodies in vinegar, salt and water for a few minutes. Drain and set aside.

Sauté garlic, onion, tomatoes and shrimp. Cook for 5 minutes. Add celery, sugar, Worcestershire sauce and vinegar. Season with salt and pepper. Simmer for 2 minutes. Cool. Stuff squid. Reattach tentacles with toothpick.

Place squid in a skillet and brush with oil. Pan fry slowly until squid turns light brown. Serve on a bed of parsley.

Stuffed *Adobong Pusit*

Pusit
Garlic, chopped
Onion, chopped
Chorizo de bilbao or bacon, chopped
Salt to taste
Del Monte vinegar
Red or white wine
More garlic
Bay leaf
Olive oil

Clean *pusit*. Remove thin covering from body and set aside to drain.

Set aside ink sac. Drain head and tentacles and chop. Mix and blend together chopped garlic, onion, *chorizo de bilbao* or bacon, chopped head and tentacles. Season with salt. Stuff squid bodies.

Cook *adobo* style in mixture of Del Monte vinegar, red or white wine (Leonora uses "*Yon tira tira*"), olive oil, bay leaf and garlic. Let boil. Add ink. Simmer till tender and dry.

In another saucepan, heat olive oil and brown more crushed garlic and add to cooked *pusit*.

Note: Most authorities say squid has to be cooked either briefly or long. Do it in between and it gets tough.

Squid *Relleno*

Squid

Filling:
Shrimp, peeled and chopped fine
Squid tentacles, chopped fine
Onions, minced fine
Tomatoes, minced
Bell pepper, chopped fine

Clean the squid. Remove head and wash bodies and tentacles well.

Cook body till tender. (Over-cooking will toughen the squid).

Sauté onions, tomatoes and add shrimp, squid tentacles and bell pepper. Cool. Stuff the body with filling. Dip in beaten egg and dredge with flour. Fry till nicely brown.

The *Guinataang Pusit* and *Ulang Ulang* are Marinduque fiesta fare former Mayor Dominador Leonida served me and my friends on a Holy Week visit.

Ginataang Pusit
Pusit, cleaned and cut into 1-inch squares
Vinegar or *dayap*/lemon/*calamansi* juice
Soy sauce
Salt
Ground pepper
Kakang gata
Garlic
Onions

Marinate the cut-up *pusit* in vinegar or its equivalent, soy sauce and pepper.

Shortly before serving, sauté generous amounts of garlic and onions in hot oil; add the *pusit*, setting aside the marinade for use later, and cook till sort of fried.

Add the marinade and simmer till thick. At this point the squid can be served as is. But for the special touch, add *kakang gata* and continue cooking till sauce is thick and oily.

Ulang-Ulang

Ulang, head removed and peeled
Shrimp juice (extracted from pounded heads and peel)
Dayap or *calamansi* juice
Garlic
Onions
Buko (from *murang dalaga* or *malakanin*)

Sauté the garlic and onions in hot oil, add the shrimps and cook till pink. Add the shrimp juice, stirring occasionally. Add the *buko* (scraped with a spoon), *dayap* or *calamansi* and season to taste.

Paksiw na Tulingan with Gata

Line pot or pan with sliced ginger. Arrange *pechay* leaves over ginger. Salt lightly. Arrange fish slices which have been salted lightly on top of *pechay*. Add a little vinegar and soy sauce. Cook till dry. Add second extraction of coconut milk to the fish. Add sliced pepper and arrange another layer of *pechay* leaves on top. Add first extraction of coconut milk and let boil. Remove from fire.

I always prepare Braised Clams during beach vacations in San Fabian, Pangasinan where I can be sure seafood is fresh and come from unspoiled waters.

Braised Clams

Add enough water to cover 1 kilo fresh clams. Add 1 tablespoon rock salt and soak a few hours to rid it of sand.

In 2 tablespoons oil, stir-fry 1 teaspoon chopped ginger, 1 teaspoon minced garlic. Add clams and cook. Add 1 tablespoon chopped green onions.

In a bowl mix 1/2 tablespoon soy sauce, 2 teaspoons sugar, 1 teaspoon sesame oil, 1 teaspoon Chinese vinegar, 2 teaspoons cornstarch and 2 tablespoons water. Add to clams and cook, stirring until slightly thick.

Gata de Cangrejo is another recipe of my cousin Nenggay Cabato of Zamboanga City. The *kangkong* or *pako* tops, I think, make the difference.

Gata de Cangrejo

1 kilo crabs
***Gata* from 2 medium-size coconuts**
2 to 3 cups *kangkong* tops or *pako* (river ferns)
Salt or *bagoong* to taste

Clean the crabs well and halve. Cook the crabs in the second *gata* and add salt or *bagoong* to taste. When the crab is cooked, add the first *gata* and let boil. Add the *kangkong* tops or *pako* and cook till vegetables are tender. Stir the mixture occasionally while cooking.

The three recipes that follow are taken from a cookbook by the well-known home economist, the late Maria Y. Orosa, that Puring and Florencio Concepcion graciously lent me. Ms. Orosa's *Rellenong Bangus* is simmered in tomato sauce, not fried nor baked.

Rellenong Bangus Espesyal

1 large *bangus*
3 tomatoes, ripe, chopped
1 onion, sliced
4 garlic cloves, crushed
1 *posuelong keso de bola*, grated
Ground pepper
Sweet peas
Green onions
1 can tomato sauce
2 eggs
Salt to taste
Cooking oil

Prepare the *bangus* for stuffing. Cook the flesh and bones in boiling water just long enough to be able to pick the bones.

Heat the oil in the skillet. Sauté the garlic, onions, tomatoes and then add the finely flaked *bangus*, season with salt and pepper.

Beat the eggs slightly, add to the sauteed bangus together with half of the sweet peas and grated cheese. Stuff the *bangus* skin and sew back, if needed.

Prepare sauce: In a saucepan, heat oil and sauté finely sliced onion. Add tomato sauce and cook for a while. Add 1 cup of broth, season to taste. Add the stuffed *bangus*, cover and cook over slow fire for about

8 minutes. Add the other half of sweet peas and the green onions.

Alimango at Togue

4 *alimango*
1 cup *togue*
Green onions
8 *sibuyas* Tagalog, sliced
1 liter rice washing
6 garlic cloves, crushed
Patis to taste

Wash the *alimango* well and cut in half.

Sauté the garlic and *sibuyas* Tagalog in hot oil till brown. Add the *alimango* and cook. Season to taste with *patis*. Add the rice washing, cover and cook for about 10 minutes. Add the *togue* and green onions. Do not overcook the vegetables.

Lauyang Dalag
(Lutong Kapampangan)

1 large *dalag*
1/2 green *papaya*, grated

1 bundle *sitaw*
4 eggplants
20 *bataw*
1 bundle *pechay*
Green onions
6 bananas, *saba*
1 teaspoon ground pepper
1 onion, sliced
4 garlic cloves, crushed
3 tablespoons cooking oil
1 1/2 liters rice washing

Clean the *dalag* well. Slice into serving pieces. Salt lightly and fry. Drain on paper towels.

Wash vegetables well and cut into bite-size pieces. Slice the bananas.

In a skillet, heat oil, brown garlic and onions. Add *papaya* and *sitaw*, eggplants, bananas. Season with salt and pepper. Add 1 1/2 liters of rice washing and bring to a boil. Add the fried *dalag*, *pechay*, green onions and *achuete* color.

Rice
&
Noodles

❄❄❄❄

Garlic Rice with *Gata* was the staple food of my Zamboanga cousins during the Japanese Occupation.

Garlic Rice with *Gata*

Cooked rice
Garlic, crushed
Salt
Thick coconut milk

Brown the garlic in a little oil. Add the rice and fry as in *sinangag*. Season with salt. When it's done add very thick coconut milk and continue cooking until the oil is extracted.

In Zamboanga, my mother used to tell me, no fiesta was complete without *pancit sotanghon*. The secret of my mother's *sotanghon* was that she used *bagoong alamang*, the juice extracted after pounding it in a mortar, to flavor it. Unlike some cooks who use carrots and green beans for their *sotanghon guisado*, my mother's version was all *sotanghon*.

Sotanghon, Zambo Style

Sotanghon
Garlic, lots of it
Onion
Patis
Pork *liempo*, cooked and cut into small bits
Shrimp, peeled
Chicken, cooked and shredded
Shrimp juice
Chicken broth
Salt and pepper
Green onions
Bagoong alamang, juice extracted

Soak *sotanghon* in water or chicken broth.

Sauté lots of garlic, pounded fine, till brown and crisp. Set aside.

Sauté onion, add the shelled shrimp and cooked pork and chicken meat.

Add the shrimp juice and *bagoong* juice and simmer for a while to get rid of its fishy taste. Add the chicken broth, let boil, then add the cut up sotanghon.

Season with *patis* and pepper to taste.

To serve garnish with browned garlic and green onions.

Pancit Palabok

Shrimp, *halabos*, peeled
Tinapa, scales removed and shredded fine
Chicharon, finely chopped
Garlic, finely chopped (lots of it)
Achuete soaked in a little amount of water
Shrimp juice (from shrimp heads and peel)
Cornstarch
Duck's egg
Salt or *patis*
Aligue
Noodles for *palabok* or second class *bijon*
Green onions, finely chopped (optional).

Prepare the sauce: Work the *achuete* seeds soaked in a small amount of water with fingers to get the color out. Repeat for as long as there is color obtained from it or when you have enough colored water. Set aside.

Pound shrimp heads and peel, add water and strain to get juice.

Brown the finely chopped garlic. Add the *achuete* coloring and the shrimp juice. Let boil. Add the cornstarch dissolved in a little water and let boil. Add beaten duck's egg in a stream, stirring all the while. Season to taste.

Brown more garlic. Set aside some for garnishing. Add the *aligue*. Add to the first mixture.

Cook the noodles: Boil water. Drop in the noodles and cook till done. Do not overcook. Drain and arrange on serving platter. Pour enough sauce to cover noodles. Arrange the shrimp over the sauce and drizzle with the *tinapa* and *chicharon*. Garnish with chopped green onion and browned garlic. Serve with *calamansi* juice and *patis*.

Pasta is one great dish and it takes only 15 minutes to prepare. What's more, it is low in sodium. What makes it fattening is the rich sauces. But today you can have your pasta with low fat sauces.

Jack Denton Scott in "The Complete Book of Pasta" says you could serve two different pasta dishes a day without repetition all year long. And for more variety, it comes in over 150 shapes and sizes.

To cook pasta:
* Use 7 quarts water for every pound of pasta.
* Use a very deep kettle or Dutch oven so the pasta has enough room to swim around without bumping into each other.
* Add 2 tablespoons of salt, just before you add the pasta.
* After adding the salt turn up the heat to keep the water boiling and gently add the pasta, being careful not to break it. Push down the pasta with a wooden fork until it is submerged. Once it boils lower heat to medium.
* Occasionally use wooden fork to separate strands.

Never use a spoon because this will bring the pasta together.

* Do not cover pasta during cooking.

* Test for doneness: The larger the pasta, the longer the cooking. But you must test and test again. Trust only your teeth – *al dente*. And start testing early. Pasta is done when it is "biteable," firm without being chewy, and with no flavor of flour.

* Reduce cooking time by about one third when the pasta is to be cooked again in a casserole.

* Fresh pasta cooks quickly. Have sauce prepared and the table set before you put the pasta in boiling water.

* Add 1 1/2 tablespoons olive oil to boiling water to prevent the fresh pasta from sticking.

* Fork long strands of pasta from the pot, directly onto serving plates or into a warm bowl of butter.

* For shapes other than strand or noodles, like shells, elbows or rigatoni, you may use a slotted spoon or quickly pour the pasta into a colander, then very quickly into butter in a bowl.

To serve:

* Never place a lot of sauce on pasta. Toss pasta in butter, add a small amount of sauce and toss again, and when it is on the individual serving plates add a large spoonful of sauce in the center and the cheese just before serving.

* Remember, the pasta should not wait for the diner; the diner should wait for the pasta.

To eat:

James Beard says what we all know—pasta is not a mannerly food. You can twist it around your fork or use a spoon if it helps. A spoon is good for getting up the sauce left at the bottom of the bowl or plate.

* If you slurp the few strands that are bound to hang loose, do so without embarassment—the best way to eat pasta is with gusto.

One last word: Fresh pasta hardly swells at all. Dried pasta doubles in volume when cooked.

Classic Cream and Egg Sauce

Melt 1/4 cup butter or margarine in a small saucepan. Sauté 1 large onion, chopped (about 1 cup) until soft; remove pan from heat. Beat 2 egg yolks slightly in a small bowl with fork; beat in 1 cup light cream or milk. Stir into butter-onion mixture and return pan to burner. Heat slowly, stirring often, but do not boil. Season with 1 teaspoon salt and a dash of ground nutmeg. Pour over pasta, add 1 cup grated Parmesan cheese.

20-Minute Tomato Sauce

Heat 1/4 cup olive oil in a medium-size pan. Stir in medium-size onion, chopped (1/2 cup), 2 medium-size carrots, pared and finely chopped, and 1 clove garlic, minced. Cook, stirring, 10 minutes, or until vegetables are soft. Stir in 1 can (1 pound) stewed tomatoes, 2 teaspoons salt, 1 teaspoon mixed Italian herbs, crumbled, and 1/4 teaspoon freshly ground pepper. Heat to boiling; lower heat and simmer for 10 minutes.

Garlicky Butter and Oil Sauce

Melt 1/4 cup butter or margarine in a small saucepan. Sauté 1 large onion, chopped (1 cup), and 2 cloves garlic, minced, in butter until onion is soft, but not brown. Add 1/2 cup chicken, beef or clam broth and 1/4 cup olive oil and heat slowly for 3 minutes. Stir in 1/4 cup chopped parsley, 1 teaspoon salt and 1/4 teaspoon freshly ground black pepper. Note: You can substitute 1 bunch leeks or green onions, trimmed, washed well and sliced, for the onion.

Velvety Bechamel Sauce

Melt 1/4 cup butter or margarine in a small saucepan; sauté 1 small onion, chopped (1/4 cup), in butter until soft; stir in 3 tablespoons all-purpose flour, 1 envelope or teaspoon instant chicken broth and 1/4 teaspoon pepper with a wire whip. Cook, stirring constantly, until mixture bubbles, 3 minutes. Stir in 2 cups milk with a wooden spoon and cook, stirring constantly, until sauce thickens and bubbles for 3 minutes.

You don't have to limit your pasta dishes to these basic sauces. There are delicious extras to go with the basic sauce of your choice of pasta shape—ziti or lengths of macaroni, shells, linguine or flat spaghetti, fettuccine or folded noodles, egg noodles, bow ties, fusilli or twisted spaghetti, very thin spaghetti, rigatoni or wide macaroni, to name a few.

Recipe #1

Wash and trim 10 ounces fresh spinach; place in a large skillet with water on leaves; cover. Bring to a boil; turn off heat and let stand for 2 minutes; drain very well. Chop coarsely. Add to pasta with sauce and 1/2 cup crumbled cheese. Toss until cheese melts.

Recipe #2
Sauté' 1 cup diced salami in a small skillet until brown; push to one side; add 2 cups thinly sliced eggplant. Cook, stirring constantly, 5 minutes, or until crisply tender; taste and season with salt and pepper. Add 1/4 cup sliced stuffed olives and heat for 2 minutes, or until pasta is cooked; then toss with pasta and sauce.

Recipe #3
Sauté 1/2 kilo chicken livers, halved, in 2 tablespoons butter or margarine in a medium-size skillet for 5 minutes; push to one side. Cut 1/2 pound trimmed fresh asparagus or green beans into 1-inch pieces; add to skillet and cook for 5 minutes; or until crisply tender. Toss with pasta and sauté in kettle.

Recipe #4
Combine 1 package (10 ounces) frozen peas with 2 tablespoons butter or margarine and 1 tablespoon water in a small saucepan; bring to a boil; cover, simmer for 5 minutes. Stir in 1 cup thinly diced prosciutto or boiled ham and 1 teaspoon leaf basil, crumbled, and sauté for 3 minutes. Add to pasta with sauce and toss.

Recipe #5
Halve, seed and dice 1 red and 1 green pepper. Drain oil from 1 can (6 1/2 ounce) tuna into a small skillet; sauté' diced pepper in oil for 5 minutes, or just

until crisply tender; flake tuna into skillet and heat for 2 minutes. Add to kettle with 1/2 cup grated Parmesan cheese and toss well with sauce.

Recipe #6
Drain liquid from 1 can (7 ounces) salmon into a small skillet. Pare and thinly slice 1 medium-size cucumber; add to skillet and cook, stirring often for 5 minutes, flake salmon into skillet, removing skin and bones. Heat slowly with 1/4 cup nuts for 3 minutes. Add to pasta with sauce and toss to blend. Sprinkle with ground black pepper.

Recipe #7
Heat 1 tablespoon olive or vegetable oil in a small skillet; sauté 2 cups sliced zucchini for 2 minutes; add 1 cup sliced pepperoni and sauté for 3 minutes, or until zucchini is crisply tender. Add to kettle with 1 cup cubed mozzarella cheese and tomato sauce and toss until cheese melts.

Recipe #8
Cook 1/4 cup sliced almonds or cashew halves in 2 tablespoons butter or margarine in a small skillet until golden; push to one side; add 2 cups thinly sliced raw broccoli and sauté 3 minutes; or until crisply tender; add 1 cup julienne pieces baked ham and cook 2 minutes. Add with sauce to pasta in kettle.

Recipe #9

Melt 1 teaspoon butter or margarine in a small skillet; add 1 to 2 cups cubed cooked beef and 1 large green pepper, halved, seeded and diced. Cook, stirring often, until pepper is crisply tender and meat is heated through. Add to kettle with sauce and 1 cup shredded cheese.

Recipe #10

Sauté' 4 sliced frankfurters in 2 tablespoons butter or margarine in medium-size skillet; add 10 ounces cooked lima beans and 2 tablespoons water; cover skillet; cook for 5 minutes. Add to pasta and sauce with 1 cup cubed process American cheese and toss until cheese melts.

USA Macaroni Bake

1 16-ounce package elbow macaroni
2 tablespoons olive or salad oil
1 large onion, diced
1/4 teaspoon pepper
250 grams cooked ham, cut into 1 by 1/4
    inch pieces
1 tablespoon all-purpose flour
1 1/4 cups milk
2 cups sharp cheddar cheese, shredded
1 14 1/2 to 16-ounce can tomatoes, drained
    and coarsely chopped

1 8-ounce container low-fat cottage cheese
1/4 cup dried breadcrumbs
2 tablespoons butter or margarine, softened

Preheat oven to 350°F. Grease a 2 1/2-quart casserole. Prepare macaroni as label directs; drain.

Meanwhile, in a 12-inch skillet over medium heat, in hot oil, cook onion and pepper until onion is golden and tender, stirring frequently. Add ham and cook until ham is golden, stirring occasionally. Add flour and cook for 1 minute, stirring constantly. Gradually add milk to skillet, stirring to loosen brown bits; cook until mixture boils and thickens slightly. Remove skillet from heat.

Reserve 1 cup shredded cheese for topping. Into skillet, stir tomatoes, cottage cheese, cooked macaroni and remaining cheddar; spoon into casserole.

In a small bowl, mix breadcrumbs, margarine and reserved cheddar cheese until mixture resembles coarse crumbs. Sprinkle topping over macaroni. Bake, uncovered, 20 minutes or until topping is golden brown and macaroni is heated through. Makes 6 servings.

W hat ingredients go into the making of a *paella*?
     Oil: Olive oil, of course.
     Rice: Either long-grained or the round variety-Japanese rice, California rice. But local *milagrosa* and *dinorado* are just as good.

Meat: Chicken, pork (salt pork, bacon or ham) or chicken livers. A must is *chorizo bilbao*.

Seafood: Prawns, lobsters, clams, mussels, crabs, squid (bodies only, discard heads and ink), any white fish, or even the lowly *tulya*, mainly for its broth to be used in cooking the rice.

Vegetables: Peas, lima beans (*patani*), stuffed olives or red and green bell peppers. *Pimiento morones* is a must.

The paella we are most familiar with has tomatoes (canned; or fresh, blanched, seeded and peeled) but it can also do without. Then the saffron or turmeric gives it a distinct yellow color.

Spices: Saffron, turmeric or paprika.

Saffron is the threadlike filament of a special variety of the purple crocus. These delicate filaments have to be carefully picked by hand and is the world's most expensive spice. There are only 3 filaments per flower and it takes 250,000 filaments to make 1 pound. It is sold in tiny strands called threads or as a powder. Anyway, you need only a pinch of it or 1/8 to 1/4 teaspoon per recipe.

For garnish: you will need hard-boiled eggs, lemon wedges and sprigs of parsley.

Utensils: You will need a *paellera*, a low-rimmed round pan usually made of cast iron from which it is also served. In case you don't have one, a large skillet with oven-proof handles will do. My late cousin Lu, in fact, used to use a rectangular stainless steel pan with sides no higher than 2 inches for her *paella* good for 25 servings.

The basic procedures for most recipes are almost the same.

Lu's *Paella*

Brown the salt pork or slab bacon, sliced thick, in the olive oil. Set aside.

Pat dry the chicken cut into serving pieces and brown in the same oil and bacon drippings. Set aside.

Either cook the prawns in olive oil or cook in a small amount of water as in *halabos na hipon* and save broth.

Boil the rest of the seafood, each separately, and save the broth. Cut crabs into 4 pieces, squid into rings and remove half of the shells of each clam and mussel. Set aside.

Reduce olive oil in skillet where chicken and pork were browned and sauté 1 head of garlic, crushed; 1 big onion, chopped. Add 2 medium cans of whole tomatoes or 2 kilos of ripe fresh tomatoes, blanched, seeded and peeled; 2 cans of tomato paste; 3 tablespoons of rock salt; 12 to 14 cups liquid (chicken broth and broth from boiled shellfish plus water to make the required amount); 5 cups California rice (do not wash); and 3 tablespoons paprika. Cook till almost done, stirring lightly occasionally.

Transfer to *paellera*, arrange on top, chicken, bacon, fish, prawns, clams, crabs, 1 big can of *pimiento morones*, sliced, and *chorizo bilbao*, sliced diagonally, and cooked sweet peas.

Cook in 350°F oven for about half an hour or till rice is cooked.

Try to time your cooking so final cooking in the oven starts about 30 minutes before serving.

Nenggay's *Paella*

Chicken, cut up
Lean pork, cut into cubes
Garlic
Onion
Tomatoes
Olive Oil
Rice
Chicken broth
Shrimp
Potatoes, pared, cut into quarters
Sweet peas
Turmeric
Pimientos

Sauté garlic, onion, 2 tomatoes. Add pork and cook for a while; then add the chicken. Cook, covered, till half-done.

In another saucepan, sauté garlic in olive oil. Add rice and cook till slightly toasted. Add chicken mixture and chicken soup broth. Add raw shrimp, sliced potatoes, sweet peas; then add enough turmeric to turn the rice yellow. (It takes very little.) Cook over slow fire, covered, till rice and shrimp are done. Stir once or twice, if necessary. Top with sliced *pimientos*.

Vegetables

❄❄❄❄

These so-called KPMS recipes, meaning dishes made of *kadyos*, *papaya*, *malunggay*, and *sigarilyas*, come from all over the country and were compiled by the Home Economics Division of the Bureau of Agricultural Extension of the Department of Agriculture.

This compilation was generously shared with me by fellow-Soroptimist Amadea Medina who was with the BAE all her active professional life.

The *kadyos*, rich in protein, may either be fresh green pods or the dried beans. Green *papaya* on the other hand, is a good source of Vitamin C and some vitamins A and B. *Malunggay* leaves and pods are rich in iron, calcium, Vitamins A and C. *Sigarilyas*, or winged bean, is considered the wonder vegetable. It is rich in protein and vitamins. What is not commonly known is that its tuberous roots are also rich in protein.

For meatless days, *tokwa* can be substituted for the pork in the recipes.

Kadyos with Blanched *Dilis*

1 medium-size onion
4 medium-size tomatoes
6 cups rice washing
2 cups *kadyos* (fresh or dried)
Salt to taste
1 cup blanched *dilis*

Peel and slice onion. Cut tomatoes into cubes. Add to rice washing together with the *kadyos* seeds. Simmer till *kadyos* is tender. Season to taste. Add the blanched *dilis* and let boil for another 5 minutes.

Sautéed Young *Kadyos*

2 tablespoons oil
3 cloves garlic
1 medium-size onion, sliced
1/2 cup tomatoes, sliced
2 tablespoons soy sauce
1 cup *dilis*
1 cup squash, sliced
1 cup young *kadyos* pods
2 cups *malunggay* leaves
Salt to taste

Sauté garlic, onion, tomatoes. Add *dilis*, squash and *kadyos*. Cover pan and cook for 10 minutes. Add *malunggay* and continue cooking for 3 minutes. Season to taste with soy sauce. Serve hot.

Kadyos Guisado I

1 cup *kadyos*
2 tablespoons oil for sautéing
2 cloves garlic
1 small onion
2 medium-size tomatoes
8 medium-size shrimp
1/4 cup pork or *tokwa*, cubed
1/2 cup shrimp juice or pork broth
Salt or soy sauce to taste

Blanch *kadyos* seeds, continue simmering until seeds become tender. Sauté garlic, onion and tomatoes. Add shrimp and pork or *tokwa*. Add the cooked *kadyos*. Add the broth and season to taste. Cook for 3 minutes.

Kadyos Guisado II

1 head garlic
1 onion, sliced
1/2 cup tomatoes, sliced
1 cup *kadyos*, boiled tender
1/2 cup shrimp, peeled and sliced in half
1/2 cup cooked pork, sliced
1 cup *papaya*, sliced
1 cup *sigarilyas*
1 cup potatoes, sliced
2 cups *malunggay*

2 tablespoons cornstarch
Salt to taste

Sauté garlic, onion and tomatoes. Add *kadyos*,
shrimp and cooked pork slices. Add *papaya*, *sigarilyas*
and potatoes and cook till tender. Add a little water,
cook for 3 minutes. Add *malunggay* leaves. Dissolve
cornstarch in a little amount of water and add to
cooked vegetables. Serve hot.

KPMS with *Dilis* and Coco Milk

1 cup coconut milk, second extraction
1 cup dried *dilis*
1 tablespoon *bagoong*
1 cup squash, cubed
2 cups fresh *kadyos*
1 cup green *papaya*, cut into cubes
1/4 cup red pepper
1 cup *sigarilyas*, cut into 2-inch lengths
1/4 cup sliced tomatoes
1/2 cup pure coconut milk, first extraction
1 cup *malunggay* leaves

Heat second extraction of coconut milk with dried
dilis and *bagoong*. Cook for 10 minutes.

Add squash and cook for 3 minutes. Add fresh *kadyos*, green *papaya*, red pepper, *sigarilyas*, tomatoes. Cook for 4 minutes. Add thick coconut milk and *malunggay* leaves. Serve hot.

Dried beans, peas and lentils have many things going for them. They are rich sources of low-fat and low-cholesterol protein, and contain thiamine, magnesium, phosphorous, potassium and zinc. To top it all, they are packed with water-soluble fiber which lowers blood cholesterol levels. As if that were not enough to convince us to serve them often, they are cheap and make great eating, too. Halo-halo wouldn't be the same without them, don't you agree?

Except for split peas and lentils, dried beans have to be soaked prior to cooking to restore moisture and shorten cooking time.

Overnight soaking in water 3 times their volume produces beans of more uniform texture which cook faster.

Other points to keep in mind:
* Generally speaking, beans should be precooked before being combined with other ingredients.
* Change soaking water 2 to 3 times to get rid of the sugars in beans which cause gas. This will cause some loss of water-soluble vitamins and proteins, but there will be enough to spare.
* To cook beans, simmer, not boil them.

* Salt and acidic ingredients like tomatoes should be added only toward the end of cooking time; otherwise, beans will take longer to tenderize.

* As with pasta, beans should be cooked *al dente*, tender but firm enough to keep their shape. In soups or purees, however, firmness is not necessary.

* When eaten with grains, beans produce 30 percent more protein

Macaroni and Beans

1 1/4 cups drained pinto beans
1/4 pound salt pork, chopped
1/2 cup chopped onion
1 clove garlic, finely chopped
1 can (1 pound) stewed tomatoes
1 can (8 ounces) tomato sauce
1 1/2 teaspoons salt
1/8 teaspoon pepper
1 teaspoon dried basil leaves
1 package (8 ounces) elbow macaroni

Wash beans. Turn into medium bowl; cover with cold water. Refrigerate, covered, overnight.

Next day, drain beans. Turn into large saucepan. Cover with 4 cups water; bring to a boil. Reduce heat and simmer, covered, 1 1/2 hours.

Drain.

When the beans have cooked about 45 minutes, sauté salt pork in medium skillet until melted and browned. Add onion and garlic and sauté until tender. Add stewed tomatoes, tomato sauce, salt, pepper and basil; bring to a boil. Reduce heat and simmer, covered for 30 minutes.

Meanwhile, cook elbow macaroni. Drain well. Combine beans, tomato sauce and macaroni; toss lightly to combine well.

Homemade Baked Beans

2 cans (28 ounces each) pork and beans
1 medium-size onion, chopped fine
1 medium-size green bell pepper, finely
       chopped
1/4 cup tomato ketchup
1/4 cup packed brown sugar
2 tablespoons prepared mustard

Heat oven to 350°F. Mix all ingredients in a deep 2- to 3-quart casserole until blended. Bake 35 to 45 minutes until bubbling.

Soybeans with Banana Blossoms and Coconut Milk

1 cup boiled soybeans
1 cup thin coconut milk
1 cup finely chopped banana blossoms
4 cloves garlic
Ginger
2 tablespoons *bagoong*
1/2 cup thick coconut milk

Boil the thin coconut milk with *bagoong*, garlic and ginger. Slice the banana blossoms and add to coconut milk. Cook for 3 minutes. Add beans, then the thick coconut milk. Cook for 3 minutes longer.

Fresh *Lumpia*

1/4 kilo pork *liempo*, boiled and sliced
1/2 kilo shrimp, shelled
1/2 head medium-size cabbage, shredded
1 onion, sliced
Garlic, crushed
Peanuts (ground or chopped) for garnishing
Soy sauce
Kinchay, cut into half-inch lengths
Kamote, medium-size, julienne

1 cup string beans, sliced diagonally
1 carrot, julienne
3 tablespoons cooking oil
2 squares *tokwa*, cut into cubes
Lumpia wrappers (recipe follows)
Lettuce leaves
Paalat (recipe follows)

For the filling: Sauté the garlic and onions. Add the shrimp and pork. Add the *tokwa*. Add the carrots, *kamote*, string beans and lastly, the cabbage and *kinchay*. Do not overcook the *kamote*, nor the other vegetables. Season to taste and cool before wrapping.

Lumpia wrapper:
1 duck's egg, slightly beaten
1/4 cup cornstarch
Dash of salt
1/2 cup water
Little oil

Mix all ingredients till smooth. Use about 1/4 of batter for every crepe. Use a non-stick pan, lightly oiled. Turn the pan around to spread the batter thinly. Cook only one side. Stack the crepes as they cook, separating them with wax paper.

Paalat:
Caramelize brown sugar in a heavy saucepan, stirring continuously until sugar is completely melted and caramelized. Take care not to scorch the sugar.

Add a little water and simmer till the caramel is dissolved. Add cornstarch which has been dissolved in water and *toyo*. Stir continuously until mixture is cooked to a smooth transparent consistency.

To make *lumpia*:

Put 2-3 tablespoons of filling in *lumpia* wrapper, roll and seal. Serve with *paalat* and ground peanuts.

Fish Balls with *Pechay*

1 *bangus*, scaled
Onion, finely chopped
Cornstarch
Green onions
1 egg, beaten
Salt and pepper
Patis
Pechay
Mami noodles

Loosen the flesh from the bones of the fish by pounding on fish with flat blade of knife. Slit the back and remove the flesh. Pick out small bones. Place in a mixing bowl.

Add the chopped onion, cornstarch, green onions (save some for garnishing), egg, seasonings. Mix well. Form into 1-inch balls.

Prepare the fish stock by boiling the head, bones

and skin of the *bangus* in 3 cups water. Strain into a saucepan.

Boil fish stock and drop in fish balls one at a time. Add the *mami* noodles and *pechay*; cook till done. Do not overcook noodles. Season to taste.

Ginataang Santol

Peel *santol* thinly and remove seeds. (About 30 to 50 *santol*). Soak in water. Boil *santol* in water. When it's soft, remove from water and squeeze out remaining water. Slice 1/2 kilo of pork (*kasim*), peel 1/2 kilo of shrimps and pound peel for shrimp juice.

Sauté tomatoes, garlic and onion. Add shrimp juice, pork and shrimps, and cook till tender. Add *santol*. Add bell pepper. Add first extraction of coconut milk and boil.

Togue with Liver

1/4 kilo pork liver
Soy sauce
Wine
Pepper
1/4 kilo *togue*
Garlic
Onions

Mix the soy sauce, wine and pepper for the marinade.

Marinate the liver, cut into strips, for 20-30 minutes.

Clean the *togue*, wash well and drain in colander. Heat a little oil in saucepan and sauté garlic. Add the *togue* and season with salt. Cook for about a minute. Remove from fire and put into a serving plate.

In the same saucepan heat a little oil. Sauté garlic and onions, then add the marinated liver. Stir and cook till done, covered. Pour over *togue* and serve hot.

Part II

Kusina ni EC

Part II

Adobo

❄❄❄❄

My sister-in-law's mother Nana Itang not only made the best San Miguel, Bulacan delicacies but was also an innovative cook. For souring Adobo, she used green mangoes or *sampaloc*. Summertime before Annapolis became part of Greenhills, she would gather *salagubang* from our backyard. In fact, her grandchildren assigned to the provinces would bring her *salagubang* for *pasalubong*.

Adobo with Green Mangoes

1 kilo pork
Green mangoes
Soy sauce
Salt
Pepper
Garlic

Cut the pork, part *kasim*, part *liempo*, into cubes. Pare the green mangoes and cut the meat into strips.

Cook the pork in the rest of the ingredients till pork is tender, the green mangoes mushy and the sauce thick.

Be sure to cook more rice for the day's meal when you serve this dish.

Adobo with *Sampaloc*

You'll need the same ingredients as for the above; just use *sampaloc* instead of green mangoes.

Boil the *sampaloc* in a small amount of water and mash well to extract the juice.

Cook the *adobo* using this for souring.

Adobong Hipon

1 kilo shrimps/prawns
Lard
Vinegar
Soy sauce
Peppercorns
Salt
Garlic, pounded

Peel the shrimps, leaving tails and heads intact. Marinate in vinegar, soy sauce, peppercorns, salt and garlic mixture.

Heat lard and when it is hot, add the shrimps and marinade and cook till shrimps are cooked.

The heads are just irresistible and so long as your cholesterol level is normal, you can indulge yourself.

Adobong Salagubang

Live *salagubang*, wings and legs removed
Soy sauce
Vinegar
Salt
Garlic
Ground pepper

Cook all ingredients together until mixture is dry. Brown some garlic in oil, add the cooked *salagubang* and fry till crisp.

*A*dobo *sa Gata* was shared by my friend Elayda Marasigan whose mother used to cook up this dish in the family home in Pagsanjan, Laguna. Today, this is one of my favorite preparations for shank, the other being *Cocido* and *Osso Buco*.

Adobo sa Gata

1 kilo *kenchi*, whole or sliced
Salt, garlic (lots of it), ground pepper, a little sugar
Vinegar
Gata (thick, fresh; or medium, using instant *gata*)

Cook your kenchi as you would your adobo and add the gata when the meat is almost tender. Cook till the oil comes out.

Cook Aqui who has been with the Olives family since she was a young girl prepares this *Adobo* for her boss, Monset. She'd wrap it up in banana leaves as topping for rice, long before Toppings became a fad.

Aqui's *Adobo*

Chicken, cut into serving pieces
Pork *pigue*, cut into serving pieces
Vinegar
Soy sauce
Garlic
Pepper, ground

Marinate chicken and pork in marinade of vinegar, soy sauce and pepper.

Heat oil; brown garlic, add chicken and pork and brown. Separately boil the marinade with a little water and pour over chicken and pork. Simmer till dry and meats are tender.

Pork *Adobo* with Beer

1 kilo pork
Garlic
Peppercorns
Soy sauce
1/4 cup vinegar
1/2 cup beer (drink the rest)

Cut pork into serving pieces and marinate in next five ingredients for at least an hour.

Cook in a saucepan till tender. Simmer till dry and oily.

Chicken *Adobo* with *Gata*

Chicken, cut in serving pieces
Garlic
Pepper
Salt
Ginger
Vinegar
Laurel leaves
Soy sauce
Gata

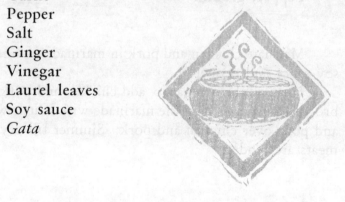

Cook the chicken together with the rest of the ingredients except the soy sauce and *gata*. When the chicken is almost done, add soy sauce. Add thick coconut milk and continue cooking until just before the oil is extracted.

Hawaiian *Adobo*

1 kilo lean pork
1 head garlic, crushed
1/4 cup vinegar
1 cup water
2 tablespoons soy sauce
Salt and pepper to taste
1 #2 can pineapple tidbits, drained
Syrup from pineapple tidbits

Cook pork with garlic, vinegar, water, soy sauce and salt and pepper to taste. When pork is tender, add pineapple syrup and cook till mixture becomes syrupy. Add pineapple tidbits and cook 3 minutes longer.

BABY FOOD

❋❋❋❋

Kusina ni EC

Cooking for the baby is much easier for mothers today than it was a couple of years ago. Gone are the days when most mothers, especially working mothers, had to depend on commercial baby food.

With food equipment like blenders, food mills and baby food grinders, today you can prepare fresh, healthier, instant baby food for your baby.

The baby food grinder, in particular, is a boon for mothers, being really convenient and versatile. It will grind fruits, vegetables and meat, and in small batches, just enough for each meal. Which means baby gets fresh, nourishing food right from the table. It's so small and light, you can take it along when traveling or dining out, so that babies can enjoy dinners with the rest of the family. Because it can grind almost anything, your baby can enjoy a greater variety of food and learn to eat almost anything.

Your pediatrician will tell you what food to give your baby and when. What I've done for you is put recipes together for the time when your baby is ready for certain foods.

Some points to remember:
* If you can't grind it, don't feed it to your baby.
* Don't force any food on your baby. He will eat what you feed him when he's ready for it. Baby knows best.
* If you're preparing beans, be sure to throw away the skin of the beans that collect under the cutting blade.

* If you're serving baby food from family dinners, set aside baby's portion before seasoning it for the rest of the family.

* Introduce new flavors and textures gradually.

* Because meat and poultry have grainy texture when pureed, it is best to combine them with some other food so they will slip down easily.

* Start baby's solid food with soft food (cereals, pureed fruits) and proceed to junior dinners (food with coarse texture such as vegetable and meat processed in the baby food grinder) and toddler dinners (mashed or chopped food which may include some pureed or ground food).

Dilis Powder

Remove heads and stomach of dried *dilis*. Toast 1 cup *dilis* over slow fire 20 to 30 minutes. Grind or pound *dilis* very fine and pass through sieve to strain. Repeat grinding or pounding and straining through sieve 2x or 3x more. Keep in a clean, dry bottle.

To use: Add *dilis* powder to *lugaw*. (Good for babies 6 months or over).

Squash with Egg

2 tablespoons cooked squash, mashed
1 tablespoon milk
1 egg yolk from soft boiled egg
Salt to taste

Blend all ingredients well and cook for 3 minutes over medium fire, stirring constantly.

Good for babies 6 months and over. For 5-month-old babies, strain before serving.

Toddler Omelet

1 egg
1 tablespoon milk
1 1/2 teaspoons unsalted butter
1/4 cup any pureed vegetable

Beat egg slightly. Add milk. Melt butter over low fire. Pour egg mixture into pan. Cook slowly over low heat, carefully lifting sides with a spatula to let uncooked part run underneath. When done turn onto serving plate. Heat vegetables and spread on top of cooked egg. Fold in half.

Pureed fruit, meat or shredded cheese may be used in place of vegetables. The fruit and meat may be diced if the toddler can handle it.

Mashed Potatoes

Puree cooked potato and add hot milk. Beat until fluffy. Heat pureed vegetables and serve in the center of a mound of pureed potato.

For toddlers: Use diced vegetables instead of pureed ones. Diced meat or cheese can also be used in place of vegetables.

Fish

Grind or mash deboned fish from *sinigang*, *pesa*, *tocho* or *sinuam* (for 4 to 6 months).

For 6 months and over, debone and flake fish from same sources.

Egg Soup

Grind 2 tablespoons cooked rice. Add 1/2 cup chicken or beef stock and let boil. Add 1 beaten egg yolk, 1 tablespoon milk and 1/4 teaspoon salt. Simmer for 3 minutes.

Pureed Vegetables

Puree steamed vegetables like broccoli, green and wax beans, celery, spinach, mustard leaves or parsley. Puree vegetables like squash from *bulanglang*, potatoes or sweet potatoes from *linaga*, *mongo* from sautéed *mongo* and add to *lugaw* and season with salt.

Pureed vegetables can also be added to ground beef and other dishes.

Pea, Bean and Lentil Puree

1 cup any legume, uncooked
3 cups water or skim milk
1 tablespoon butter or margarine
1/4 cup milk

Pre-soak beans overnight in stockpot. Add butter to pot to prevent foaming over. Simmer, partly covered, also to prevent foaming over, until legumes are done. Skim off any skins that float on top for a smooth puree.

Puree with any equipment, adding milk to thin a little.

Vegetable and
Egg Yolk Custard

Blend together in medium-size bowl 1/4 cup vegetable puree, 1 large egg yolk, beaten, 1/4 cup whole milk and 1/2 teaspoon brown sugar. Pour into custard cups and cook on top of half-cooked rice.

Mushrooms

1 pound fresh mushrooms
1 tablespoon butter/ margarine, optional
2 tablespoons wheat germ, rice or instant
    cereal

Wash mushrooms thoroughly. Leave stems but cut off tough ends. Steam caps and stems on top of a double boiler or sauté in butter for 5 to 10 minutes. Puree mushrooms and their juice in blender or baby food grinder. Add the thickener after pureeing the mushrooms.

Leche Flan

Blend 1 beaten egg, 1/4 cup evaporated milk, 1/4 cup water and 1 tablespoon sugar. Strain into small container that can be placed on top of half-cooked steamed rice.

Baon

❄❄❄❄

Here are a few do's and don'ts:

* Choose food the child likes. Common sense tells us this is the number 1 dictum. Anton, my grandnephew, for example, likes Cebuano *longanisa* but doesn't like the Ilocano version. So why serve him with the latter?

Who cares to see untouched lunchboxes and a cranky kid with a grumbling stomach at the end of the school day?

* Choose food that doesn't spoil easily. This explains why *adobo*, fried chicken, fried pork chop and fried *ewan*, invariably appear on the food list of families where packed lunches are a part of the lifestyle.

* Strive for variety. Remember, it's the spice of life.

Take fried chicken. You can vary the seasonings. You can marinate the chicken in a mixture of *toyo-calamansi*, *patis-calamansi*, salt and pepper, 5 spice etc. It can be fried "a la Max" or floured and breaded "a la Kentucky." But, though I've given you at least 4 marinades for fried chicken, I wouldn't recommend you serve these Mondays to Thursdays!

When Bebot V. was in grade school, his mother confesses, she was rather preoccupied with her ailing elderly parents and left the matter of packed lunches and snacks to her maid Conching. Day in and day out of peanut-butter-jelly sandwiches left Bebot with an aversion to it.

* If the kid's lunch is last night's dinner, make sure to set aside his portion before the family sits down

to dinner. This way the kid doesn't get the impression that his lunch is tira or leftovers.

* Don't worry too much about the problem of keeping food hot. It's good for the kids to learn to eat cold lunches, says Tess C., mother of Amina and 2 boys, all with hearty appetites.

There are many kinds of insulated lunchboxes in the market but she finds them all unsatisfactory.

Cold food can be a problem with finicky eaters, though.

* Don't worry either about the kid's required vegetable intake. These could come in the form of garnishings for all the fried whatnots that make up most lunchboxes menus. They can have extra generous servings of their favorite vegetables at dinner time.

* Don't be afraid to serve saucy dishes. They won't spoil. But do stay away from greasy food.

* Don't serve food like squid or fresh garlic unless your kid can brush his teeth somewhere. You don't want him sporting blackened teeth or spewing deadly garlic breath within a radius of 1 foot and repelling his seatmate and teacher, do you?

* Tuck in a surprise treat every day. This could be a favorite cookie, a slice of fruit in season, a small bag of *chicharon* or caramel popcorn, sealed to keep it crisp. Children love food that crackle and pop.

* If it's at all possible, get the kids to help prepare the food. This advice comes from a nutritionist from Cornell U who says it's the best way to get kids to eat healthy food.

Helping could be as simple as stringing the beans, crumbling the bacon, shaping the fish balls or peeling the *saba* bananas for the *Arroz a la Cubana*.

* Lastly, pack the food attractively. Use small containers. If it's too big, the contents will get all sloshed up and look like Miss Piggy's lunch. Take a cue from the Japanese who are known for their exquisitely prepared lunchboxes.

Breakfasts

Cottage Cheese Pancakes

1 cup small curd cottage cheese
4 eggs
1/4 cup flour
Dash of salt
1 cup applesauce

In a bowl, beat until fairly smooth cottage cheese, eggs, flour and salt (there will be small lumps of cottage cheese). On lightly greased hot griddle or skillet, cook scant 1/4 cup batter until golden on both sides, turning once. Remove to warm platter. Repeat with remaining batter. Serve with applesauce.

Sour Cream Pancakes

1 cup sifted all-purpose flour
1/2 teaspoon double-acting baking powder
1/2 teaspoon baking soda
1/2 teaspoon salt
1/2 cup dairy sour cream
1/2 cup milk
2 eggs
3 tablespoons butter or margarine, melted

Sift flour with baking powder, soda and salt. Combine sour cream and milk, stirring well.

In a large bowl of electric mixer, at high speed, beat eggs until light and fluffy. At low speed, alternately blend in flour mixture and sour cream mixture, beginning and ending with flour. Then blend in the melted butter.

Meanwhile, slowly heat griddle or heavy skillet. Use a scant 1/4 cup batter for each pancake; cook until bubbles form on surface and edges become dry. Turn; cook 2 minutes longer, or until nicely browned on underside. Serve with whipped butter, strawberry sauce or hot maple syrup. (Recipes follow.)

Griddlecakes

1 cup sifted all-purpose flour
2 teaspoons double-acting baking powder
1/2 teaspoon salt
2 tablespoons sugar
1 egg
1 cup milk
3 tablespoons butter or margarine, melted

Sift flour with baking powder, salt and sugar into medium bowl. With rotary beater, beat egg. Add milk and butter; beat until well mixed. Pour into dry ingredients; beat only till combined—batter will be lumpy.

Meanwhile, slowly heat griddle or heavy skillet. Use about 1/4 cup batter for each griddlecake; cook until bubbles form on surface and edges become dry. Turn; cook 2 minutes longer, or until nicely browned on underside. Serve with Whipped Butter or any of the sauces given below.

Banana Griddlecakes: Sift 1/8 teaspoon nutmeg with Griddlecake dry ingredients. Add to batter 1 cup mashed bananas and 2 teaspoons lemon juice. Serve with Whipped Butter or any of the sauces given below.

Whipped Butter: Let 1/4 pound sweet or salted butter stand at room temperature in small bowl of mixer for 30 minutes. Beat at low speed until smooth; then beat at high speed until light and fluffy. Serve at room temperature.

Strawberry Sauce

12 ounces strawberries, sliced
2 tablespoons cornstarch
1 teaspoon lemon juice

In medium saucepan, combine 1 tablespoon water and the 2 teaspoons cornstarch; then stir until smooth. Add remaining ingredients; bring to a boil, stirring. Sauce will be slightly thickened and translucent. Serve the sauce warm.

Hot Maple Syrup

1 cup dark brown sugar, firmly packed
1/4 teaspoon maple flavoring
2 tablespoons butter or margarine

Combine brown sugar and 1/2 cup water in medium saucepan; bring to boiling. Boil uncovered for 5 minutes. Add maple flavoring and butter; stir until butter melts. Serve hot.

Croissant French Toast

2/3 cup milk
3 eggs
1/3 cup orange juice
1 teaspoon sugar
1 teaspoon vanilla
1 teaspoon grated orange peel
1/4 teaspoon ground cinnamon
1/8 teaspoon ground nutmeg
4 day-old croisssants, halved lengthwise
1 stick unsalted butter
Confectioners' sugar
Maple syrup

Whisk first 8 ingredients in medium bowl. Add

croissant to egg batter and turn until thoroughly coated. Melt butter in large heavy skillet over medium-high heat. Add croissants and cook until golden brown on both sides, about 3 minutes per side. Sift confectioners' sugar over. Serve with syrup.

Rum Raisin French Toast

3/4 cup raisin ice cream
3 eggs, beaten to blend
1/3 cup ground walnuts
1 tablespoon rum
1/4 teaspoon cinnamon
8 slices raisin bread

Combine melted ice cream with next 4 ingredients in large shallow pan. Dip raisin bread into ice cream-egg mixture and let soak for 1 minute per side. Melt 2 tablespoons butter in heavy skillet over medium heat. Place 4 bread slices in skillet and cook till brown. Repeat with remaining batter and bread. Serve immediately with maple syrup and more ice cream.

Banana French Toast

Banana bread cut in 3/4-inch slices
4 large eggs
1/4 cup whipping cream
2 tablespoons brown sugar
1 teaspoon vanilla extract
1/4 teaspoon each ground nutmeg and
    ground cinnamon
3 tablespoons butter
Maple syrup

Whisk together eggs, whipping cream, brown sugar, vanilla, nutmeg and cinnamon in large bowl until blended. Melt 1 tablespoon butter in heavy, large skillet over medium heat. Place some bread in batter and turn to soak thoroughly. Add bread to skillet. Cook until golden brown on both sides. Transfer to cookie sheet; place in oven to keep warm. Repeat with rest of ingredients. Serve. Pass syrup separately.

Cooking
in
Aluminum
Foil

❄❄❄❄

What could be more appealing than a meal wrapped in banana leaves? A meal wrapped up in silver— aluminum foil.

I have always used banana leaves for wrapping up my working lunch and also resorted to it on picnics. It was only when I had to start watching my figure (or disfigure?) that I chanced upon cooking with aluminum foil. You know what diet experts say about the 3 B's for weight watchers — baking, boiling, broiling.

My oven is too big for 1 or 2 packets of meals and boiling doesn't appeal to me except for a few dishes. Broiling, on the other hand, involves too much trouble cleaning up unless you use one of those smokeless grills, which doesn't appeal to me either.

I tried wrapping up my chicken or fish dish in aluminum foil and cooking it on a rack in a cast iron *kawali*. I had chanced upon a baking-steaming method that served me well till the *kawali* sprang a leak.

Next I tried cooking my foil packets on a rack in a stainless steel skillet with a little water and it did just well.

Actually, cooking in foil is nothing new. It was just that, in my case, I discovered it on my own.

Why do I claim cooking in foil is more appealing than cooking in banana leaves or corn husks for that matter?

Foil does not "breathe" and, therefore, allows a great amount of steam to accumulate inside the packet. Moisture is sealed in.

For people who don't like the flavor banana leaves and corn husks impart to food cooked in them, foil doesn't impart a taste of its own which makes it a good alternative. In fact, the flavors of the different ingredients do not meld such that carrots taste like carrots and corn like corn.

Other advantages of cooking in foil:
* Foil is strong and easy to work with and can be sealed tightly and neatly.
* Because it is neat and presentable, it can be served as it is with the packet placed on one's dinner plate.
* Packets can be prepared in advance, refrigerated, and reheated shortly before serving time. This ensures you not only of a piping hot meal but also time to enjoy the latest from the talk shows.
It is ideal for working people who stagger home tired and hungry.
Many times when I was working full time, I'd tell myself on the way home that I'd just gulp down a glass of milk, take a shower and creep into bed. When I was home at last, however, hunger would see me whipping up something more substantial.
* It is specially helpful for you people on a diet because putting one serving in each packet means you can control your portion size and leaves no room for second helpings.
* Cleaning up is easy because all you have to do is wrap up what's left of the chicken or fish, if it is not deboned, in the same piece of foil.
* Food will not brown and even overcooking

won't dry up the food, as in other methods.

Not all kinds of food, however, can be successfully cooked in foil. Chicken, fish, vegetables and other light, quick-cooking foods suitable for steaming work well. In general, meats do not steam well, except for lean cuts like chicken, pork and turkey cutlets and boneless pork loin.

To prepare packets:

* Cut a piece of aluminum foil large enough to hold the ingredients with room to fold over and seal. Cutting too small or too large a piece of foil is a waste. Foil is expensive. If it's too small, you'll have to cut a piece of foil the right size, not just make up the difference. It is essential that the foil used is in one piece.

* Cut ingredients into even-sized pieces.

* Some recipes recommend lightly oiling the foil. I don't add the extra fat; I don't need it.

* Assemble the packets starting with the main ingredient—fish, chicken etc. and topping it with vegetables and sauce, if any.

* Hold opposite ends of the foil and fold over at least twice for a tight seal. Seal the shorter ends neatly and tightly.

To cook:

* Preheat oven to hot (500°F) and bake-steam packets for the time specified in the recipes.

* In stainless skillet cooking, I start with high heat and lower it to medium low when the skillet is

hot. Cooking time is 15 minutes for fish, 1 hour for chicken or pork.

* You can open packets to check for doneness and reseal. But take care you don't get steam-burned.

* Be precise about cooking time. It may mean the difference between not quite done, cooked to perfection or overdone.

To serve:
* Place packets on individual dinner plates. Puncture the seal by making an X on top and pulling back each section to reveal the hidden treasure. Breathe in deeply to savor to the fullest the aroma released. Dig in.

The *bangus*, *tanguigue* and pork chop recipes are very simple and what I usually cook for myself. My chicken recipe is a complete meal in itself.

Chicken in Foil

1 broiler chicken, quartered
Salt and pepper
Onion, minced
Potatoes, quartered
Carrots, cut in chunks
Sweet peas
Miniature corn
Button mushrooms

Season the chicken with salt and pepper.

Place chicken, skin side down, in the middle of the foil big enough to be sealed. For less cholesterol, remove skin. Add vegetables.

Fold the two long ends of the foil together and fold again sealing securely to keep the juices from leaking out.

Cook on rack in a *carajay* or stainless steel skillet over medium-low heat when the pan is heated through. Do not turn, otherwise you will lose the juices.

Variations, using different seasonings:

Five-spice powder
Curry and a little milk
Soy sauce and *calamansi*

To make your own five-spice powder: Mix 1 teaspoon ground cinnamon; 1/4 teaspoon fennel seed; 1/4 teaspoon pepper; 1/8 teaspoon ground cloves. Makes about 2 1/2 teaspoons of five-spice powder.

Bangus in Foil

1 *bangus*, scaled, sliced at the back and cut into
    3 portions—head, belly and tail
Onion, minced
Tomatoes, chopped
Ginger, minced
Salt

Mix the onion, tomatoes and ginger. Season with salt. Season *bangus* lightly with salt. Stuff each portion with the vegetable mixture. Wrap in foil and seal well. Cook in rack in a *carajay* or stainless steel skillet covered, for about 15 minutes.

Tanguigue in Foil

Tanguigue slices, lightly salted
Onion, minced

Place *tanguigue* slices on foil. Top with minced onion. Cook on rack in *carajay* or stainless steel skillet, covered, over medium high heat for about 15 minutes.

Cooking
with
Beer

❄❄❄❄

Paksiw na Pata with Beer

1 pork *pata*, cut up
1/2 cup vinegar
Brown sugar to taste
1/2 cup dried banana blossoms
Laurel and oregano leaves
1 clove garlic, crushed
Salt, soy sauce and pepper to taste
4 *saba* bananas, fried
1 cup beer

Soak banana blossoms in water and remove hard tips. Clean *pata* well. In a saucepan cook the *pata* in the beer and enough water to cover it. Add the rest of the ingredients except the *saba* and cook till tender.

Just before removing from the fire add the *saba* bananas.

Beef in Beer Sauce

1 1/2 kilos chuck
3 tablespoons corn oil
2 cups sliced onions
1 1/4 teaspoons salt
1/2 teaspoon freshly ground pepper
1/8 teaspoon thyme
1 1/2 cups beer
1 tablespoon sugar
1 tablespoon vinegar

Trim all the fat from the beef and cut into 2-inch cubes. Heat the oil in a heavy saucepan or Dutch oven; brown the onions and beef in it. Add the rest of the ingredients, cover and cook over low heat till meat is tender. Skim the fat.

Prawns a la San Miguel

1/2 kilo prawns
1/4 cup cornstarch
1/4 cup cooking oil
4 stalks leeks, cut into 1-inch pieces
1 cup tomato sauce
1/2 cup San Miguel Beer
1/2 cup water
3 tablespoons sugar
1 teaspoon salt

Snip off tails and legs of prawns and cut in back lengthwise. Dredge with cornstarch and fry in hot oil till crisp. Set aside.

Sauté leeks and add tomato sauce, water, sugar and salt. Add beer and simmer until sauce is almost thick. Add the fried prawns and continue simmering till almost dry. Serves 8-10.

Shrimp Boiled in Beer

**4 cans or bottles (12 ounce each) beer
1 tablespoon salt
2 1/2 kilos fresh medium shrimp in shells
Cocktail sauce**

Heat beer and salt to boiling in Dutch oven. Add shrimp. Heat just to boiling; reduce heat. Cover and simmer 3 to 5 minutes or until shrimps are pink. Drain. Serve with cocktail sauce.

Cocktail sauce: Mix 1/2 cup ketchup, 2 tablespoons lemon juice and 2 to 3 teaspoons prepared horseradish.

Cooking Light

❄❄❄❄❄

Even if we have to watch our calories and cholesterol intake, we don't have to give up our favorite family recipes. All we have to do is pick out the "problem" ingredient, those that are harmful to our health, and find substitutes for them. Or eliminate them altogether, if necessary. And we can use healthier methods of cooking like baking, boiling, broiling or stir-frying. Charcoal broiling, however, is not too good for us either so we'd better forget our desire for the smoke flavor it brings and use the oven instead.

Shop for the leaner cuts of beef and pork, serve more fish, poultry, vegetables, and fruits; remove chicken skin before cooking; cook dishes with soups or sauces a day ahead and skim off the fat the following day before serving; use more egg whites than yolks when eggs are called for in a recipe; use low-calorie soy sauce and salt-free tomato sauce; use herbs for flavoring.

These are some of the tips given for healthy diets.

Oven-Fried Chicken

2/3 cup packaged plain breadcrumbs
1/2 teaspoon each celery salt, onion
    powder, paprika and dried thyme
1 broiler-fryer, cut in quarters
3 tablespoons plain low-fat yogurt

Heat oven to 400°F. Place a wire rack, large enough to hold the chicken, in a baking dish or pan.

Line dish with foil for easy cleanup.

Pull skin off chicken and cut off excess fat. Use fingertips to coat chicken with yogurt. Press chicken in breadcrumb mixture (mix crumbs and seasonings). Turn to coat completely. Place on rack, leaving space between pieces.

Bake 45 to 50 minutes until coating is lightly browned and juices run clear when meat is pierced with the tip of a knife.

Note: A thin coating of yogurt is all that's needed to make the crumbs adhere. Baking the chicken on a rack ensures that chicken is crisp all the way around.

Curried Chicken

2 tablespoons dry nonfat milk
2 tablespoons flour
3/4 teaspoon curry powder
2 cups skim milk
Onion, salt and pepper
2 pimientos, chopped
Mushrooms, chopped
2 cups diced cooked chicken

Over very low fire, lightly brown nonfat milk powder in saucepan. Add flour, curry powder and a small amount of liquid milk, stirring until smooth.

Add remaining milk and cook, stirring till thickened. Season with onion salt and pepper. Add remaining ingredients and heat through.

Spaghetti with Eggplant Sauce

3 tablespoons corn or soya oil
1 big eggplant, cut into cubes (do not peel)
1 onion, sliced
1 clove garlic, minced
1 green pepper, sliced
1 cup chopped tomatoes, seeded
1 cup tomato juice
1 teaspoon oregano
2 teaspoons basil
12 ounces spaghetti noodles

Heat oil in Dutch oven over medium heat. Sauté eggplant about 7 minutes. Add onion, garlic and bell pepper. Sauté until tender, about 3 additional minutes.

In a bowl combine tomatoes, tomato juice and herbs. Add to eggplant mixture. Reduce heat, cover and simmer 1/2 hour. Cook spaghetti, drain and combine with eggplant sauce before serving.

Sesame Soy Chicken

1 cup finely chopped onion
1/2 teaspoon fresh lime juice
1 teaspoon grated lime rind
1/4 cup light soy sauce
1/3 cup sherry
2 tablespoons grated fresh ginger
1/4 cup orange juice
1 tablespoon sugar
3 cloves garlic, minced
1 tablespoon hot pepper oil
6 chicken legs and 6 chicken thighs,
    skinnned, all visible fat removed
1 tablespoon sesame seeds, toasted

In a bowl combine onion, lime juice, rind, soy sauce, sherry, ginger, orange juice, sugar, garlic and oil. Set aside.

Rinse chicken and pat dry. Arrange in a baking dish and pour lime mixture over, turning each piece to coat completely. Cover with plastic wrap and refrigerate several hours or overnight, turning chicken pieces twice during that time.

Preheat oven to 400°F. Bake chicken with marinade 35 minutes, turning pieces in cooking juices to maximize flavor. Sprinkle with sesame seeds before serving.

Yogurt

❄❄❄❄

A dairy product that is gaining more and more popularity these days is yogurt. Tart, piquant and delicious, it can be used for recipes calling for sour cream, milk or buttermilk and it has fewer calories, besides.

While commercially made yogurt is available, you can make your own at less cost and you don't need any special gadget to make it. All you'll need is a little amount of starter — too much will result in a sour, watery product.

Some points to remember when making yogurt:

- Place all your equipment where you can leave your yogurt-in-the-making undisturbed for 5 to 8 hours. Yogurt doesn't care to be disturbed while it's growing.

- Add the starter to the milk gently.

- Make sure the bacteria that create it are kept warm but not too warm. If the milk to which you add your starter is too hot, the bacteria will grow faster, but the curd will be too thick and rather tough.

- Keep it covered and in a warm place away from drafts while it's growing.

- Yogurt should be ready in 5 to 8 hours.

- It is ready if the contents have reached a custard-like consistency. To test, tilt bowl to see if contents hold together.

- The longer you incubate the yogurt, the more sour it will be.

- Reserve a small quantity to use as starter for your next batch.

- Refrigerate yogurt. In three hours, it will firm up even more.
- Don't store in freezer. Large crystals will form. But there is such a thing as frozen yogurt.

To make yogurt:

You will need 1 quart milk, 2 tablespoons nonfat dry milk powder and 2 tablespoons plain commercial yogurt (or 3 to 4 tablespoons if yogurt is not absolutely fresh).

Mix milk and milk powder in heavy saucepan. Bring to boiling over low heat, stirring constantly. Pour mixture into warmed bowl and cool to lukewarm before adding yogurt. (Check temperature of milk by sprinkling a few drops on inside of your wrist.) With small whisk beat in yogurt, stirring until smooth. Pour mixture into four clean 7- to 8-ounce jars with lids, cover and keep warm (110°F to 112°F) in any of three ways: 1. If your oven has a pilot light, wrap jars in a dish towel and place them upright in a pan in the oven. 2. Put jars in a pot of lukewarm water and cover it. Replace water as it cools. 3. Wrap jars in a heating pad turned to lowest setting. Whichever method you use, yogurt should be ready in 5 to 8 hours. When mixture is the consistency of thick cream or thin custard, refrigerate. Makes about 1 quart.

More points to remember:
* In cooking, add yogurt to the mixture slowly and do not overstir or it will lose its body and become thin.

189

* Do not allow yogurt mixtures to boil unless flour is used in the recipe.

* If you prefer to buy commercial yogurt, buy it plain and stir in your favorite fresh fruit.

Commercial fruit yogurts contain sugar or corn syrup to help preserve the fruit. Two grams of plain, low-fat yogurt contains 72 calories; the same quantity of low-fat with fruit yogurt, 230 calories.

Yogurt Mashed Potatoes

2 pounds russet or baking potatoes, pared
    and cut into
      1-inch cubes (about 5 cups)
2 1/2 teaspoons salt
1 cup low-fat plain yogurt or skim milk
2 tablespoons unsalted butter, melted

Cover the potatoes in a large saucepan with cold water. Add salt. Bring to a boil. Cook for 10 to 15 minutes or until fork tender. Drain and return to saucepan.

Meanwhile, preheat oven to broil if you wish to brown top of potatoes.

Add yogurt to potatoes. Mash with potato masher or hand mixer (texture will be slightly different).

Using pastry bag fitted with decorative tip, pipe potato into flame-proof 9-inch pie plate or similar shallow baking dish; form decorative design on top with fork. Drizzle with melted butter.

Broil for 3-6 minutes or until lightly browned, if you wish.

Yogurt Dinner Rolls

1/4 cup warm water
2 tablespoons sugar
1 package active dry yeast
1 cup plain nonfat yogurt
2 tablespoons corn oil or margarine
1 egg
1 teaspoon leaf oregano
2 teaspoons basil
2 tablepoons grated onion
3/4 cup whole wheat flour
3/4 cup all-purpose flour
1/2 teaspoon salt
1/2 cup all-purpose flour
3/4 cup whole wheat flour

Combine sugar and yeast and add warm water. Set aside for 5 minutes or until bubbly, then add yogurt and melted butter or margarine, egg, oregano, basil and onion. Beat with electric mixer at low speed for 30 seconds. Beat for 3 minutes on high.

Sift together 3/4 cup all-purpose flour and 3/4 cup wheat flour and 1/2 teaspoon salt. Blend into yogurt mixture. Stir in rest of flours. Dough will be moist and sticky.

Lightly oil a large bowl with corn oil. Add dough, turn once to coat evenly. Cover with towel and let rise 1 1/2 hours. Punch down and form 18 balls. Lightly spray a 9 x 13-inch baking pan with vegetable oil. Arrange balls in pan. Let rise for 40 minutes. Preheat oven to 400°F. Bake for 15 minutes.

Yogurt Pancakes

4 eggs
1 container (8 ounces) vanilla low-fat yogurt
1/4 cup water
1 cup all-purpose flour
1 tablespoon baking powder

Over medium heat, preheat large skillet or griddle, greasing if necessary. In medium sized bowl with wire whisk, lightly beat eggs. Stir in yogurt and water until blended. Add flour and baking powder, stirring well until just combined (do not overmix).

For each pancake, pour 1/4 cup batter onto hot griddle and cook about 2 minutes or until edges are dry and bubbles appear on the surface. Turn and cook other side until golden. Serve hot, garnished with fresh fruit and syrup. Makes 12.

Yogurt Dressing

1 cup yogurt
2 tablespoons white vinegar
1 1/2 tablespoons lemon juice
1/8 teaspoon freshly ground pepper
2 tablespoons chopped chives
2 tablespoons finely chopped parsley
Salt to taste

Combine all ingredients and blend well. Refrigerate.
Variations:
Honey Yogurt Dressing: Add 2 tablespoons honey and omit the chives and parsley.
Yogurt and Mayonnaise Dressing: Add 1 cup mayonnaise.

For Kiddie Cooks

✳✳✳✳

When I was a kid my cousin Med and I used to spend many hours making mud pies and decorating them with aratiles — early versions of the Black Forest Cake. We remember fondly how my father would pause from his many preoccupations to take a "bite" of our creation and lick his lips in appreciation.

Later I had lots of fun shaping bread dough for dinner rolls my godmother would bake for her family.

Today my three and four-year old grandnieces spend many quiet, peaceful hours stirring imaginary ingredients in their miniature pots and pans and asking us grownups to "taste" their cooking.

Kids indeed love cooking and summer vacation is a good time to do something to nurture this. Of course there are lots of schools offering cooking lessons for kids, but there is nothing like doing fun things together as mother and daughter or son. Quality time, *ika nga*.

But you don't just let your kids loose in the kitchen. You prepare them for the activity by citing some do's and don'ts. You stick around and supervise the kids' activity. In cooking lessons for younger children, you actually do the cooking, assigning the kids simple tasks such as fetching pots and pans, tearing the lettuce for a salad, mixing ingredients in a bowl, shaping meatballs or bread or cookie dough. Older children can measure ingredients including pouring liquid ingredients, cutting margarine into pastry flour. Everybody can brush melted margarine over pastries and breads, shape cookies with cutter. The important thing to remember is to keep the tasks within each child's abilities.

Some reminders for adults:
* Never leave children alone and unsupervised in the kitchen when they're cooking.
* Make sure they wash their hands before and after handling food especially raw food such as poultry and eggs.
* Don't let younger children use electrical outlets.
* Allow only older children to use knives, scissors and electrical appliances.
* Keep an eye on children of all ages near ranges and keep smaller ones away from heat of any kind.

Teach the kids to:
* Use clean dry oven mitts for holding pot handles when stirring, picking up pots from the stove, to take things in and out of the oven.
* Turn all pot handles on top of the stove towards the center and never let them stick out over the ege of the stove where they may be accidentally bumped and burn or scald somebody.
* Use a wooden spoon, a metal spoon or plastic spoon (for teflon pots and pans) with a wooden or plastic handle, for stirring the contents of a pot. Metal-handled spoons may get too hot to handle, literally.
* Lift the lid off a pot away from the face to avoid getting the hot steam on their hands or face.
* Never plug or unplug an electrical appliance with wet hands or barefooted.
* Set aside knives and blender and food processor blades to be washed separately, and wash these carefully to avoid getting cut with sharp blades.

Old-Fashioned Flapjacks

3 eggs
1 cup sifted all-purpose flour
3 teaspoons baking powder
1/2 teaspoon salt
2 teaspoons salt
2 teaspoons sugar
1 teaspoon light brown sugar
1/2 cup buttermilk
1 tablespoons butter, melted

Sift the flour, baking powder, salt and sugar together. Beat the eggs till light and fluffy. Add the flour mixture to the beaten eggs and beat till smooth. Stir in buttermilk until combined. Do not overbeat. Use 1/4 cup batter for each flapjack.

Corn with Franks

1 cup potatoes, pared and diced
1 onion, chopped
Franks, cut diagonally
1 can (16-ounce) whole kernel corn, drained

Sauté diced potatoes in oil until golden brown and tender. Add chopped onion and franks. Cook and stir till franks are brown on edge. Stir in the corn. Add salt and pepper to taste. Heat through.

Tuna a la Queen

1 can cream of mushroom soup
1/2 cup milk
1 can flaked tuna, drained
1 cup cooked sweet peas
1 tablespoon chopped pimientos

Blend cream of mushroom and milk. Add the tuna, sweet peas and pimientos. Serve over toast or macaroni and bake with cheese.

Macaroni Italian Style

2 cups elbow macaroni, uncooked
1 chopped onion
1/2 cup chopped green pepper
1 clove garlic, minced
1/2 cup cooking oil
3 cups tomato juice
1 teaspoon salt
1/4 teaspoon pepper
2 teaspoons Worcestershire sauce

Sauté macaroni in oil till macaroni is golden. Add tomato juice and seasonings. Cover and simmer 20 minutes until macaroni is cooked.

Baked Potatoes in Foil

Scrub 8 baking potatoes. Brush with salad oil, if desired, for soft skins. Wrap each potato securely in heavy-duty foil.

Adjust grill 4 inches from prepared coals. Place potatoes at edge. Cook, turning frequently with tongs, 45 to 65 minutes, or until tender.

To serve: Unwrap potatoes carefully to avoid getting burned by the hot steam. Slash top of each in an X; then gently squeeze to fluff up potato. Season with salt, butter and pepper.

Fresh Lemonade

3 lemons
3/4 cup fine sugar
Ice cubes
Mint sprigs

Wash lemons well. Slice crosswise into very thin slices. Discard ends and seeds. Put lemon slices in bottom of large bowl or sturdy pitcher. Add sugar. With potato masher or wooden spoon, pound lemon slices until they are broken and sugar is dissolved. Add 1 tray of ice cubes and 2 cups cold water. Stir until very cold.

To serve: Pour lemonade, along with lemon slices, over ice cubes in tall glasses. Garnish each with a mint sprig. Serves 4 to 6.

A child expert says yeast baking is "perfect quality time": it includes conversation, making a mess and watching a mini miracle as yeast changes play dough into something delicious.

Some tips from test kitchen experts of Fleischmann's Yeast:

* For a small child who can't reach a countertop, set up his or her play table in the kitchen. Or use a sturdy step stool with non-slip top and feet for the child to sit on.

* Assign parts of the job to each child — for instance, adding an ingredient, kneading or rolling out the dough. Or cut off a little of the dough for each child to knead and never mind if the dough gets black in the process.

* Give an older child the responsibility of being a "recipe monitor." He or she can read each step of the recipe as the process unfolds and can double check the quantities and timing.

* Keep safety in mind at all times. Keep the little ones away from the range or oven. Make sure they can't pull heavy bowls or boards from countertops.

*Keep sharp knives away from small hands.

This refrigerator dough recipe that follows does not require dissolving the yeast separately. It does not require kneading. There goes half the fun of bread making. The fun is punching the dough before shaping into desired forms. Shaping the dough is lots of fun.

The whole procedure if done in one go will take about 4 hours and 40 minutes, which might be too long for a child's attention. So you might want to make it in steps.

Day 1: Prepare the dough. Refrigerate, covered.

Day 2: Punch down dough, divide and form into shapes. Bake.

Day 3: Decorate. (Bears can be frozen before decorating).

Make-Ahead Refrigerator Dough

4 1/2 to 5 cups all-purpose flour, divided
1/2 cup sugar
2 packages active dry yeast
1 teaspoon salt
3/4 cup milk
1/2 cup water
1/2 cup butter or margarine
2 eggs at room temperature

In large bowl, combine 1 1/2 cups flour, sugar, yeast and salt. In a small saucepan over medium heat, heat milk, water and butter until very warm (120°F to 130°F); butter does not need to melt. With electric mixer at low speed, gradually add milk mixture to dry ingredients. Increase speed to medium and beat 2 minutes, occasionally scraping bowl. Add eggs and ½ cup flour; increase speed to high and beat for 2 minutes, occasionally scraping bowl. With spoon, stir enough additional flour to make stiff dough. Place in well-greased bowl, turning to grease top. Cover with plastic wrap and refrigerate for 2 hours or up to 3 days.

Punch down dough; turn onto lightly floured surface. Divide and form into desired shapes.

Teddy Bread Family

Double quantity Make-Ahead Refrigerator
    Dough
Dark seedless raisins
1 egg
1 tablespoon water

Prepare dough as recipe directs.

Grease cookie sheets. Remove about 2/3 of dough; form into ball and divide in half for 2 large bears. Divide remaining 1/3 dough in half; use 1/2 for medium bear and divide remainder for 2 small bears.

For each bear, use 1 piece of dough as divided above and shape as follows:

Divide each dough piece in half. Form 1 piece into a smooth round ball for body. Place on prepared cookie sheet; flatten slightly. Divide remaining piece in half; break small piece of 1/2 for nose. Form the rest of this piece into a smooth round ball; place above larger ball to form head. Attach nose to head. Divide remaining dough piece into 6 equal parts. Shape into balls and attach to bear to form paws and ears; pinch all adjoining seams to seal. Press raisins into head for eyes and into body for belly button on Daddy Bear and Baby Bear. Make indentation in head to form mouth. Cover, let rise in warm, draft-free place about 50 minutes or until double in bulk. (The bears are lying down).

Preheat oven to 350°F. In a cup, beat eggs and cold water; brush on breads. Carefully redefine shapes if necessary. Bake for 20 to 30 minutes, or until golden brown. Remove from oven; cool completely on wire racks.

If you wish to decorate the bears further use your imagination. You may use different kinds of candy like M & M's or miniature marshmallows for the Mother Bear's and daughter's necklaces. Make an apron wth white icing for mother. Use gumdrops for father's necktie and so on. This is where your creativity comes in.

To ensure success, read the recipe over carefully before plunging into this task. Or it won't be much fun.

By the way, you can use this refrigerator dough to make any form you like — Ninja turtle, deer, crocodile, dinosaur, etc. Your imagination's the limit.

Guavas

❄❄❄❄

Going to market on rainy days, you cannot escape the redolence of ripe guavas. It's time for *sinigang sa bayabas* from scratch once more, not from an aluminum foil packet.

Before I got introduced to this Tagalog dish, I remember complaining to the canteen manager of the school where I was teaching that her dishwashers should be more thorough in their job. There was guava in my *sinigang*.

She patiently enlightened this greenhorn that the *sinigang* for the day was *sinigang sa bayabas*.

In fact, she revealed, the ability to cook it was the final test for the job as far as our school principal was concerned. "How do you cook *sinigang sa bayabas*?" he would ask prospective canteen managers.

I must admit it is now an acquired taste and sometimes even when guavas are not in season and I get a yen for it, I look out for ripe native guavas to go with my *bangus*.

Sad to say a guava tree I had nurtured from seedling to fruiting had to go in the name of progress. I still mourn for it like some people do a loved pet.

Anyway, I thought all along that guavas were only used for *sinigang na bangus*. Two Tagalog cooking friends, Pining Joya and Aling Lydia, though, say it also goes with pork and beef.

Sinigang na Bangus

1 *bangus*, scaled and cut into serving pieces
Rice washing
Patis or *bagoong na alamang*
Ripe native guavas, sliced into small pieces
Talong and camote tops or *kangkong*
Sili pang sinigang

Boil about 2 cups rice washing and the sliced guavas.

When the guavas are soft, add the *talong* and when it's almost done, the *bangus* and camote tops. Season with *patis*. (Pining Joya version).

When the guavas are soft, add the *bangus*. When the eyes bulge, the fish is cooked. Add the *kangkong* and *sili pang sinigang*, cover and turn off fire. (Lydia's version).

Aling Lydia recommends the use of Chinese *kangkong*, the white stemmed variety. This, she says, is crispy.

Sinigang na Baboy/Karne

1 kilo pork or beef
Rice washing or plain water
Ripe native guavas
Calamansi, optional

Sitao, talong and *talbos ng sili, sitao o camote*
Or *sitao, gabi* and *talong*
Salt to taste

Cook the pork or beef in water till tender. Add
the cut-up guavas, the amount depending on one's
taste. When the guavas are soft, add the vegetables
starting with the ones that cook longer like *talong* and
gabi. Season to taste. You may add *calamansi* if you
want more sourness.

Pining likes the fatty cuts, like brisket while
Lydia prefers using beef with *buto-buto* and not too fat.

Pining serves *sinigang na bangus* with fried *liempo*
or squid, and the *Sinigang na Karne* with fried fish.

Lydia copes with high prices by pairing a costly
dish like *Sinigang na Karne* with low-cost food like
fried *galunggong*.

Binabayasan

3 cloves garlic
1 tablespoon native onion, chopped
1 medium-sized tomato, chopped
10 ripe guavas, seeded and chopped
1 1/2 cups string beans, sliced
6 crabs, halved or quartered
1 cup pure coconut milk
4 tablespoons sugar
3 tablespoons salt

Sauté garlic, onion, and tomato. Add the chopped guavas and crabs. When crabs turn red, add the string beans. Cook till crisp tender. Add coconut milk. Remove from fire. Add salt and sugar to taste.

Kusina ni EC

Leftovers

Fish *Cardillo*

Leftover fish
Tomatoes, sliced
Onion, sliced
Garlic, crushed
Egg
Salt

Sauté the garlic, onion, and tomatoes. Add the fried fish. Add a little water or rice washing and let boil. Simmer for a few minutes then remove from fire and beat in slightly beaten egg, stirring all the while.

Fish Croquettes

1 cup leftover fish, deboned
Garlic, crushed
Onion, chopped
Tomatoes, chopped
1 1/2 cups mashed potatoes
Salt and pepper
1 egg

Sauté the garlic, onion and tomatoes. Add the fish. Season with salt and pepper.

In a bowl, mix this with the mashed potatoes, blending well. Form into balls or ovals, dip in well-beaten egg and fry in moderately hot fire.

Fish *a la 'Salmon'*

Leftover broiled fish (like *orreles)*
Garlic, crushed
Onion, sliced
Tomatoes, sliced
Salt and pepper

Sauté garlic, onion and tomatoes. Add the flaked fish. Add a very little amount of water. Simmer till the flavor has blended. Season to taste. (Tastes like *ginisang salmon*).

Sotanghon with Squid

Leftover squid *adobo*
Garlic, crushed
Onion, sliced
***Sotanghon*, soaked in water**

Sauté garlic and onion. Add the *pusit*, cut up into small chunks. Add a little water and add the *sotanghon*. Cook over medium heat till done. Season with salt and pepper.

Ropa Vieja

Cut up leftover beef and vegetables from *Cocido*. Sauté in garlic, onions and tomatoes. Season to taste. Simmer a while for the flavors to blend. Serve hot.

Utak-Utak

1 broiled or fried fish, flaked fine
1 medium-size onion, minced
2 eggs, beaten light and fluffy
3-4 tablespoons flour
Salt and pepper to taste

Mix all ingredients well and shape into desired form. Deep fry in hot fat.

Fish *Pompons*

1 *labahita*, boiled, deboned and flaked
Salt and pepper
Minced onion and tomato
Minced garlic
1 can (small) tomato sauce
1 egg
2 tablespoons flour
Breadcrumbs

Sauté fish with 1/2 can tomato sauce. Cook till almost dry. Cool and shape into balls.

Roll fish balls in beaten egg, flour and breadcrumbs. Fry in deep hot fat till golden brown.

Sauté remaining tomato sauce with garlic and onion and serve with fish balls.

Fish Croquettes

1 cup flaked fish (*dalagang bukid, labahita*)
2 cloves garlic, finely chopped
3/4 cup milk
1 1/2 teaspoons salt
2 tablespoons butter
2 tablespoons chopped green onion
10 small potatoes, boiled, peeled and mashed
2 eggs

6 tablespoons breadcrumbs
1 pinch black pepper

Fry the garlic and onion in lard. Add the fish, salt and pepper and cook for 5 minutes. Add the mashed potatoes and milk and cook till mixture is almost dry. Add the butter and green onions and mix well. Shape into oval croquettes. Roll in lightly beaten eggs then in breadcrumbs, egg and breadcrumbs and fry in hot fat till brown.

Crabmeat Patties

3 tablespoons butter/margarine
1 teaspoon finely chopped onion
3 tablespoons flour
1 cup powdered milk
2 cups cooked crab meat
1/4 teaspoon Worcestershire sauce
1/2 teaspoon salt
1 egg, slightly beaten
1 cup breadcrumbs (or more)

Melt butter. Add onion. Add flour and cook for 1 minute. Add powdered milk and cook stirring constantly until very thick. Cool and add other ingredients except egg and crumbs. Form into patties.

Dip in crumbs-egg-crumbs. Fry till brown. Drain and serve with desired sauce.

Chicken Croquettes

Butter or oil
1/2 onion, chopped
1/2 cup chopped ham
2 cups chicken, chopped
1 teaspoon lemon juice
1/2 teaspoon salt
1/4 cup celery salt
1 cup croquette sauce
Croquette sauce:
5 tablespoons water
1/4 teaspoon salt
1/3 cup flour
Pepper
1 cup milk
Green onions
Breadcrumbs

Make the croquette sauce by mixing the butter, salt, flour, pepper and milk and cooking till thick. Sauté onion and ham; add the chicken, lemon juice, salt and celery salt and add the croquette sauce. Form the croquettes, roll in breadcrumbs, beaten egg, breadcrumbs and fry till golden.

Oldies

Old-Fashioned Chicken

1 tablespoon salad oil
1-1.5 kilos broiler-fryer, cut up
1 medium-size onion, chopped
3 tablespoons all-purpose flour
6 medium-size red potatoes, cut in quarters
Baby carrots
2 chicken-flavored bouillon cubes
1/4 teaspoon pepper
Minced parsley for garnish

Brown chicken in hot salad oil, a few pieces at a time and transfer to an oven-proof casserole.

In drippings, cook onion till browned, stir in flour, cook 1 minute. Gradually stir in 2 cups water, stirring to loosen brown bits from bottom of skillet. Cook, stirring, until mixture boils and thickens slightly. Pour over chicken.

Add potatoes, carrots, bouillon cubes and pepper into casserole. Cover and bake in 350°F oven 50 minutes or until chicken and vegetables are tender.

To serve, garnish with parsley.

Classic Spaghetti Meat Sauce

2 slices bacon, cut into 1-inch pieces
1 medium carrot, chopped
1 medium onion, chopped
1 garlic clove, minced
1/4 kilo ground beef
Button mushrooms, sliced
1 28-ounce can tomatoes (or fresh, peeled and
    seeded)
1 6-ounce can tomato paste
1 teaspoon salt
1/2 teaspoon oregano leaves
1/8 teaspoon nutmeg

In a 3-quart casserole cook bacon till crisp. Set aside. To bacon drippings add carrot, onion and garlic. Cook, covered, till tender. Add mushrooms and ground beef and cook till beef loses its pink color, stirring occasionally.

Stir in tomatoes and remaining ingredients including bacon. Cook until sauce is thickened, stirring occasionally.

Variations: Stir in 1/2 cup heavy cream and/ or 1/4 cup red wine. Cook for 1 minute till hot.

Omelets

One versatile dish which is good for the lunchbox crowd is the omelet (*torta* or *tortilla* in the dialect).

Almost anything can go into an omelet: beef, pork, chicken, fish, mushrooms, cheese, seafood, even vegetables like cabbage and green *monggo*.

Some things to remember when making omelets:
* Have all ingredients and utensils ready because speed is of the element.
* Get the right heat for cooking, hot enough to form an envelope almost at once to hold together the softer egg layer above it, but not too hot — as this would toughen the envelope before the rest of the egg cooks.
* Have the eggs at room temperature and keep the prepared filling warm.
* Any leftover food can make a good filling so long as it is not too liquid.
* Make omelets one a time, using not more than 2 or 3 eggs.
* Beat the eggs only until they are blended.
* Don't cook the omelet dry; the center should be moist, so you can start to fold and roll it when the surface is still runny.

Tortang Alimasag

6 eggs
1 cup crabmeat

1 tablespoon soy sauce
1 teaspoon salt
1/4 teaspoon pepper
1 tablespoon cornstarch
2 tablespoons oil
1 cup *labong*, cut into strips
1/2 onion, chopped
1/2 teaspoon celery, chopped

Beat the eggs in a large bowl. Add the crabmeat, soy sauce, salt and pepper and cornstarch. Heat the oil in a skillet and sauté the vegetables about 1 minute. Cool. Add vegetables to beaten eggs. Heat some oil in skillet and cook as above.

Tortilla de Cangrejo

3 large crabs, cooked, shelled, and flaked
2 cups chopped cabbage
2 tablespoons oil for sautéing
1 large onion, sliced
2 pieces dried Chinese mushrooms, cut into
   thin strips
10 *apulid* or 1 *singkamas*, cut into 1/8" slices
1/4 kilo shrimp, peeled and deveined
1 teaspoon oyster sauce
1 tablespoon soy sauce
Salt and pepper to taste

1 medium-size *patola*, cut into 1 1/2 inch
   wedges
3 dashes sesame oil
3 eggs for every omelet (recipe makes 3-4
   omelets)

Sauté the cabbage in hot oil for 2 minutes. Add
the mushrooms, *apulid*, then the crabs and shrimp.
Season with salt and pepper, oyster sauce and soy
sauce. Add the *patola* and cabbage and boil once.
Sprinkle with 3 dashes of sesame oil. Strain and set
liquid aside. Divide mixture into 3 or 4 portions to
make 3 or 4 omelets. For each omelet beat 3 eggs
slightly. Add salt and pepper.

Heat 2 tablespoons oil for each omelet. When hot,
pour slightly beaten eggs and spread over bottom of
skillet. When partly set put filling on one side so you
can fold over the other side. Serve with sweet-sour
sauce.

Sweet-Sour Sauce

1 tablespoon cider vinegar
3 tablespoons sugar
1/2 cup water
1/2 teaspoon salt
1 teaspoon oyster sauce
1 tablespoon ketchup
1 tablespoon cornstarch
2 tablespoons water

Combine first 6 ingredients. Add the strained sauce of the filling. Boil and thicken with cornstarch dissolved in water.

Shrimp Omelet

1/2 kilo shrimp, peeled, deveined,
    and coarsely chopped
1/2 cup oil
1 clove garlic, minced
1 onion, sliced
2 tomatoes, sliced
3 eggs, well-beaten
Salt and pepper to taste

Sauté garlic, onion and tomatoes in oil. Add shrimp, season with salt and pepper. Cook till shrimp is pink. Drain and set aside.

Heat oil in skillet and pour eggs, turning pan around to spread egg over bottom of pan. Pour shrimp mixture and fold over one side of egg layer, turn over once to cook the other side.

Tortilla de Camaron

1/2 kilo raw shrimp, shelled and deveined,
  chopped
4 tablespoons salad oil
2 tablespoons soy sauce
1/4 cup green onion, chopped
1/4 cup thinly sliced celery
1/2 cup bean sprouts
8 eggs
2 tablespoons beer or wine
1/4 cup water
1 teaspoon salt

Heat 2 tablespoons oil in skillet; sauté the shrimp; stir in soy sauce, onions, celery and bean sprouts. Cook for 3 minutes, stirring constantly. Remove from heat.

Beat together the eggs, beer, water and salt. Heat the remaining oil in skillet. Pour eggs and when partially set pour shrimp-vegetable mixture over half and fold other half over it. Cook until delicately browned.

Tortilla a la Cubana

1 head garlic, crushed and chopped
2 medium onions, minced
2 tablespoons cooking oil
1 70-gram can tomato sauce

1/4 kilo ground lean pork
1/4 kilo ground beef
1/2 cup bccf stock or water
1 *chorizo bilbao*, sliced into rounds
1/4 cup fried and crumbled smoked bacon
1/2 cup raisins
Salt and pepper to taste
1/4 cup cooking oil
8 eggs
Dash of salt and pepper

Sauté garlic and onions in hot oil. Add tomato paste. Simmer for 5 minutes. Add ground pork and beef. Sauté for several minutes.

Pour stock or water and continue cooking till meat is tender. Add in chorizos, bacon and raisins. Season to taste. Cook till done. Set aside.

Heat oil. Beat eggs, season with salt, pepper and pour into frying pan. Spread over bottom of pan. Cook over medium heat until egg is set and lightly browned. Spoon the filling over half of egg and fold over the other half and cook a little longer.

Dulong Omelet

1 cup *dulong*
2 eggs
1 teaspoon salt
Pepper to taste

1 onion
1 clove garlic
Oil

Wash the *dulong* carefully; sprinkle with salt and cook in its own liquid until dry. Heat oil in pan; sauté garlic until brown. Add the onion. Add *dulong* and stir. Beat the eggs; add *dulong* and cook in a little oil. Turn to cook other side or fold egg mixture into half.

Ready Mixes

✼✼✼✼✼

One way to cut down on time spent in the kitchen is to have some versatile homemade mixes on hand from which you can whip up a variety of dishes.

Take this white sauce mix recipe. You can adjust the amount of basic mix to use depending on the kind of mix you need — thin, medium or thick.

Thin is for soup with non-starchy vegetables; medium for sauces, creamed vegetables, fish, poultry, pasta or meat; thick for souffles and croquettes.

Another plus is that you use nonfat milk and can even substitute 2/3 cup of water for the 1 cup milk needed in some recipes. This is good news for those who are wary of creamed dishes.

White Sauce Mix

1 cup flour
4 cups instant nonfat dry milk
4 teaspoons salt
1 cup butter/margarine, cut up

Mix well the flour, nonfat dry milk powder, and salt. Cut in the butter or margarine until crumbly.

Put in a glass jar and refrigerate. Makes 4 cups. Will keep for two months.

White Sauce Chart

	MIX	MILK
Thin	1/3 cup	1 cup
Medium	1/2 cup	1 cup
Thick	1 cup	1 cup

Basic Sauce

Combine desired amount of mix and milk. Cook over medium heat till thickened. Boil gently, stirring for 2 minutes. Use as desired.

Cheese Sauce

Add 3/4 cup shredded cheese after mixture thickens. Stir until cheese melts.

Curry Sauce

Add 1 teaspoon curry powder to thickened sauce.

Another mix is this multi-purpose mix you can use for a variety of dishes such as oven-fried chicken, tempura, and some baked goodies.

Multi-Purpose Mix

10 cups all-purpose flour
1/2 cup sugar
1/3 cup baking powder
1 tablespoon salt
2 cups vegetable shortening

In large bowl, combine flour, sugar, baking powder, and salt; mix well. With pastry blender or two knives, cut shortening into flour mixture until mixture resembles coarse crumbs. Store airtight in cool dry place. Will keep for 3 months.

INDEX

A

Adobo, 141
Adobong Hipon, 143
Adobong Hito, 76
Adobong Hito sa Gata, 75
Adobong Salagubang, 144
Adobong Tahong, 93
Adobong Tilapia, 82
Adobo sa Gata, 144
Adobo with Green Mangoes, 142
Adobo with Sampaloc, 143
Alimango at Togue, 104
All-American Beef Stew, 31
Aqui's Adobo, 145
Azon's Ham, 41

B

Baby Food, 149
Baked Potatoes in Foil, 200
Banana French Toast, 167
Bangus in Foil, 174
Baon, 157
Basic Meatballs, 27
Basic Sauce, 235
Batter-Fried Chicken, 63
Beef, 17
Beef in Beer Sauce, 178
Beefsteak Tagalog, 24
Binabayasan, 210
Bola Bola with Brown Sauce, 26

N

O

P

Q

Quick Roast Chicken, 65

R

Ready Mixes, 233
Recipes (Sauces) # 1-10, 115-118
Rellenong Bangus Espesyal, 103
Rellenong Tahong, 91
Rice and Noodles, 107
Roast Chicken Stuffed with Curried Rice, 66
Roasted Chicken with Lemon Grass, 51
Roast Pork or Beef, 37
Ropa Vieja, 216
Royal Apahap, 78
Rum Raisin French Toast, 166

S

Sautéed Young Kadyos, 127
Sesame Soy Chicken, 185
Shrimp Boiled in Beer, 180
Shrimp Omelet, 229
Shrimps with Tanglad Leaves, 86
Sinaing na Tulingan, 79
Sinigang na Baboy/Karne, 209
Sinigang na Bangus, 209
Sinigang na Hito sa Miso, 77
Sinigang na Isda with Tanglad, 87
Sinigang na Karne, 20
Sotanghon with Squid, 215
Sotanghon, Zambo Style, 109
Soups, 3
Sour Cream Pancakes, 162
Soybeans with Banana Blossoms and Coconut Milk, 133
Spaghetti with Eggplant Sauce, 184
Spanish Sausage, 45
Squash with Egg, 152